LAST WILL
AND TESTAMENT
OF A LOVER

*The dying have a unique opportunity to set free
those whom they leave behind.*

Henri Nouwen, The Path of Freedom

LAST WILL
AND TESTAMENT
OF A LOVER

a journey through grief

CLIFFORD R. ELLIS

Moulin

Moulin Publishing Limited
P. O. Box #560
Norval, Ontario
Canada L0P 1K0

Canadian Cataloguing in Publication Data

Ellis, Clifford, 1934–
Last will and testament of a lover: a journey through grief

ISBN 1-896867-06-5

1. Bereavement – Religious aspects – Christianity.
I. Title.

BF575.G7E44 1997   248.8'66   C97-900731–3

Printed and bound in Canada

1 2 3 4 5   ML   00 99 98 97

Cover and text design by Counterpunch / Linda Gustafson
Front cover photograph by Andrew Waller

To my loving wife Colleen,
who may well be left to grieve
and then to love again,
        and
to others who must do the same

Contents

Preface   ix

To My Loving Wife   1

My Last Will and Testament, A Love-will for My Dear Rose   5

Introduction, Disclaimers and Intent   6

The Shock of My Death   9

My Funeral Arrangements   11

Take Comfort From My Funeral   13

Connections With Family and Friends   16

A Word About Family Pain   18

Reflections for Your Memories of Me   21

A Comforting Thought for Hurting Memories   24

It Is Natural to Wonder Why   26

Comfort Will Come   30

Hope Even in Your Darkest Days   34

Perhaps You Blame Me for Dying   38

Have the Courage to Choose   41

About Cleaning My Closets   44

Frustration and Anger Are Normal   48

Let Grief Pass   50

It Is All Right to Do Well Without Me   54

When You Talk to Me   56

May My Love Set You Free   61

Talking About Me   63

Recalling Our Quarrels   65

Regrets: If Only . . .   69

Peace Be with You   73

My Will Is Gone   75

When You Dread the Nights   79

View Our Relationship as a Gift   84

View All My Things as Gifts   86

Celebrate Your Life   89

If You Write to Me   92

When You Miss Me as a Friend   95

Finding New Meaning in Life   99

Feeling Whole Again   103

You May Experience My Presence   107

When You Help Another   111

You Are Beautiful   115

Longing of Our Hearts   117

Your Need for Intimacy   121

Consider Remarriage   126

A View of Life, Love, and Self   132

The Eternity of Love   136

Good-bye, My Love   140

A Summary of My Desire   144

Epilogue   146

Acknowledgments   148

Preface

People often die without final loving words for their mates. In the movie versions of death, the dying gather intimate friends about their bedsides and make a peaceful good-bye with each of them. In reality we do not like to talk about death in our society, and we die poorly by Hollywood standards. It is unlikely we would say the things our spouses need to hear even if we remained lucid until the moment of death. We leave the business of life and love unfinished.

Death is selfish. We must be unselfish while living and loving. We know that we will die and leave our loved ones behind. We prepare wills to provide for their material and financial needs, but death demands much more of our lifelong partners than a reorganization of our assets. What about the love-relationships and the emotional needs of our grieving spouses? Perhaps we need to leave behind another kind of will – one that deals with our love-assets.

The principal character, Ross, pauses in life to consider the meaning of love and the comfort of grief. This book is his love-will to help Rose through the powerful emotions that will likely follow his death. He writes with love to support her with the comforting words she will need from him in her grief. The characters are fictional but their journey is real and will be comforting to anyone who is grieving.

You can read this book as a love-will written by the lover in each of us or as comforting words for our grief. Read and celebrate this book with tears and joy and with all the emotions of grief, but also with the joy of a celebrated love.

April 1997
Clifford Ellis

To My Loving Wife

My Dear Rose,

I love you Rose. As I write this letter, our love is my most important asset. Yet I know that death will come. I know not when, only that the cycle of birth, growth, and death is all around me. It is part of the natural rhythm of nature but it may catch us unaware. There may not be any final words of love before my death, so I have prepared a love-will in which I have sorted out my understanding of love and grief and given myself to your comfort.

When you read this letter, I will no longer be physically with you, but in a sense I will always be with you. Like our marriage provided a loving place for growth, I hope my love-will provides a protected, loving place for you. As we were there for each other in marriage, may I be present for you in your grief. May you know that you are truly loved.

Perhaps I should have talked to you as I wrote my love-will and it was on my mind. I didn't because I didn't want to spoil it by explaining it ahead of time. Do you remember how I sometimes left a little love note under your pillow when I planned to be away overnight? My motives and feelings were a bit like they were at those times. Love is joyful and childlike by nature. Lovers delight when a gift is an overwhelming surprise, and I wanted my love-will to be a perfect loving surprise.

You know me better than anyone, but you may not recognize me immediately in this letter or in my love-will that follows for I will seem different. I have tried to put my cares and selfishness aside to be fully present for you as I was not always able to be in our daily life. I know that when you read this, I will be dead. I will have no cares – our "us" will be only "you." All of value in "us" is love, and that love I give you now in my love-will. May you come to know me well in my love-will, and continue to accept my love, for it will help you in your grief.

My perspective of time is different from yours. Please understand that as I write I am outside grief but you are immersed in grief and experiencing it, ever changing, moment by moment. I hope you understand my difficulty in keeping my words appropriate for your needs at any moment. However well-planned, my words may seem insensitive at times – like a conversation with a friend who has rehearsed his words for the occasion. His words play on, but fail to touch because they do not respond to new clues from your changing moments. Or, perhaps, they seem like a recited prayer from our darkness – a prayer that begins without an awareness of our present need.

My poor timing need not be a barrier between us. Do you remember our first love letters? We read them and put them aside to reread with our hearts. I suspect you still have some of them. Love letters, like my love-will, are not intended to be scanned once and discarded but rather to be savoured and cherished. As you reread my love-will over time, various parts will speak to your changing needs. If there seems to be a barrier, remember that I write from love. It is, and was, and will always be. Perhaps our love is like a faint shadow of our God who was and is and is yet to be.

How can I comfort you when I am gone and death is between us? How do I know what you would like to read in your future grief or even what I would write at that time if I could? Only, my love, that I believe in love, as I am sure you still do. When I am gone, I believe all that will matter is love, so if I write from love alone, I will surely write what I would say and what you would like to hear if I could stand beside you. I have envisioned you in grief and simply written what love has urged me to write. Grief distorts reality and I believe it needs the quiet whispers of a lover. I pray that you get these whispers from my love-will.

Perhaps finding my love-will during your first terrible days of grief will distress you. If so, put it aside, for I assure you there is nothing here that requires your attention. It is like a long love letter, and was written only to comfort you. Read my words when you need me. I have arranged my thoughts in the sequence that I think will be most helpful, but I have also labelled each section so you can flip around more easily to find me for a particular need.

It is my hope that this gift of love, which is just a small part of the love you gave me, will help tide you through the darkness of your grief. My love-will pledges my continuing love and seals my promise to be with you through your grief. It shows my concern for you, my commitment to you, and my desire to be with you. I pray that you accept it and that it comforts you.

With love always,

Ross

MY LAST WILL
AND TESTAMENT

A Love-will for My Dear Rose

Introduction, Disclaimers and Intent

In our beginnings lies our journey's end.

Kofi Awoonor

I, Ross, your loving husband and companion for many years, declare this to be my lasting will and testament for you. My only qualification for writing this love-will is my love for you.

It is wholly written by me but it is neither notarized nor witnessed. Can you imagine love in the hands of lawyers? They know little of eternity except as the time it takes to probate. How could they deal with a lover and a beloved who were one or with a contract that was devoid of "not withstanding" and "heretofore?" In any case, all their efforts would come to naught because nothing in this love-will is binding! This truth is not fine print, but, I hope, emblazoned in free spirit on every page. It prays for you and desires all for you, but is intended to be empty of my control. My disclaimer is to question and disregard anything that appears to be binding.

This love-will does not revoke any earlier will or codicil, for such legal documents deal only with my material assets, while my love-will disburses my love and is my testament to life. Nor can this will, which gives you all my love, ever be contested. Although I also left my love to our children in other love-wills, that action cannot invalidate this will because that would be contrary to the infinite nature of love. This testament may even be shared with others and leave no less for you.

Our love leaves you a widow's dower. You have all the memories, our friends and our children, and by God's grace, grandchildren and great-grandchildren. This dower of love is yours, whether or not you should remarry. All that our love produced I leave in trust for you till your death, and yet beyond, for it is only a widow's legal dower that ends at death. The very spirit that urges me to write this love-will attests that love endures forever. This truth of love is my lasting testament which I now leave with you.

I do not claim the absence of undue influence as I did in my legal will, for I doubt there can be a stronger influence than that of love. As a second disclaimer, please disregard anything that seems unloving to you, for I intend this will to be simply a gift of love. I intend to provide a place within the safe boundary of love where you can explore your past and search for your new life. I intend to help leave your inheritance of love unencumbered, so it may support you in your grief. I intend to honour and comfort you with my love-will as I help you move on in your life.

The Shock of My Death

Every man knows that he must die, but no one believes it.

Yiddish Proverb

My love, you are reading my love-will so the unmentionable happened — I really did die. Death indeed separates us and reunion is not possible, at least in this life. You understand the words, but I suspect a dreamland of emotional shock has stripped them of meaning. You may feel an emotional hell or nothing. Either extreme is normal, but you may well wonder what is happening to you. Perhaps there is a little comfort in knowing that the shock of death is normal.

If my death is sudden, you may say, "I had no idea. It was so unexpected. If I had known and had time to prepare myself…" But remember Aunt Ethel when Uncle George was terminally ill? They lived under the cloud of death for months, but his death was still unreal to her. In spite of all her thinking of it ahead of time, it was still difficult for her to believe when it happened. She had talked about his pending death and she had summoned relatives to see him. She had even dry cleaned his suit to be ready for his funeral. When he died, we tried to comfort her by saying things like "at least it was expected" and "it must be a relief that his suffering is over." We could not understand her shock because being expected and unreal seemed a contradiction. But an expected death is not much easier to accept than an unexpected one. Either way, the feelings and sense of unreality are the same for we are usually in denial.

Your sense of unreality may continue and at times you may even feel that you are outside yourself and a spectator of your own actions. Be patient and kind with yourself for your journey of grief has begun. I pray that my love-will helps you survive the emotional roller coaster.

My Funeral Arrangements

*. . . there was need for an opportunity to
spend time with the body, to reflect, and
to say personal goodbyes.*

Irene B. Seeland

We talked briefly about funerals today and that reminded me
to write this section of my love-will. Neither of us really cared
about the details of our funerals. "I won't be around to enjoy
mine," I joked.

While not knowing my wishes, you may still feel compelled to do what you think I would want. Or, perhaps, we will
make plans later that you will find impossible to carry out. If
so, remember that any plans we made were to help you. The
law understands death and gives you full responsibility for my
body. The funeral is your decision, as any lover would want it.
I assure you with all my heart that any arrangements you make
will be fine. They could not be otherwise when done out of

love. Please, in any confusion and second guessing, take this comfort: There is no burden of correct things to do for me.

Suppose that I die in the wilderness and my remains are never found, or that no one even knows of my death. I will be no less dead, and no less connected with my Maker. My passage into the next world, whatever it may be and however it may occur, relies only on God and not on you, my love, so it is impossible for you to fail me in death. I will be gone and will have no needs. After all else has passed away, love is all that remains. Please don't lose sight of this comfort. The cross of death has already been born.

We speak of paying respects. What an odd expression. Pay? Surely not like membership dues, the mortgage, or a car payment. Love is not paid for, nor earned for that matter – just a gift. And respect? Does a friend come at death and say, "Here is the respect that I owe you? I have paid my account in full." I think paying respects reflects an earlier time. People were more connected then and life was held more reverently. As a hearse passed by, strangers would raise their hats out of respect for the gift and mystery of life. I fear that people have lost their awe of life and, without that awe, paying respects has become misunderstood as a duty to the dead.

I acknowledge your love, but my funeral and all the other ceremonies are parting gifts for you, the living.

Take Comfort From My Funeral

Failure to face and to participate in these
[funeral] ritual steps is a serious mental health
hazard for those who have just sustained the
loss of a loved person.

Ned Cassem

Your first task of grief, my love, however painful, is to accept my death. Not just to see me unthinkably dead, but to feel it undeniably in your heart. It will be so hard for you, but the opposite of acceptance is denial and there is no lasting comfort in escaping reality. And so the most loving thing that I can tell you is also the most painful. When you read this, I will be dead. I wish that it were not so but it is.

This is why funeral rituals, even the most painful and heart-wrenching, are for your comfort. They show that I am indeed dead when simple words are not enough. They are command performances in which you have to take part. They flood your senses with vivid scenes of death at the funeral home, the church, and at my grave side. Sometimes you still won't believe that I am dead, but the scenes will be unforgettable. Love has many faces. Please accept that this is one of them.

It is human nature to turn away from pain and to want to be alone. I suspect that you will want to withdraw from people and the rituals. The exhaustion may make your grief seem more than you can bear. These times will pass and you will be alone. Accept for now that turning away too soon is another form of denial that only brings more pain rather than comfort. The hectic days will lead you, even force you, to go on when you would rather withdraw to suffer alone.

Nature provides its own anaesthetic – a numbness – during the first few days of grief. Attending to my funeral and other details might be harder if delayed. The people and the rituals that force you to carry an extra burden over the first rugged mile of your journey are for your comfort. People so easily miss the love in customs and see only the painful formalities.

Closure. Burial. Termination. Separation. Good-bye. A funeral underlines all of these words with powerful imagery. Again, my love, so painful for you but not cruel, just love urging you to begin your good-bye. It sets the stage with imagery and emotion for you and all my friends to make their first words and actions of parting. There is never a fond farewell in a lover's death, however long delayed, just a separation gained by tears. How crippling it can be when the first parting is not begun at the funeral. It's a paradox of life: comfort from grief and love in pain.

The first parting, although the hardest, is but the first of many. You will say good-bye to my body, but there are a thousand deaths and a thousand partings from thoughts and emotions still to come. That is grief. There is no fear that the end depicted by my funeral will quickly put me behind. I assure you that memories will survive the fire of grief that destroys the chaff of life.

Different funeral arrangements are simply variations on a theme. Funerals require a minimum of planning, and then happen quickly in expected ways. This also provides comfort: life going on with its familiar and expected customs.

A funeral, though, is more than a shutting out as in closing the casket, in cremation, or the grave. The shutting out is only the living from the dead – an ending to help in making good-byes. The other part of the funeral is an opening up of emotions. The gifts include compassion, a softening of hearts, and a reaching out of the community to support. Love with a softer face to balance the taking away with the giving.

Please accept the comfort provided by my funeral: the truth of my death, involvement rather than withdrawal, the scenes for a first good-bye, and the drawing together of a supporting community.

Connections With Family and Friends

*Seeing His mother and the disciple He loved
standing near her, Jesus said to His mother,
"Woman, this is your son." Then to the disciple
He said, "This is your mother." And from that
moment the disciple made a place for her
in his home.*

John 19:26–27

Jesus connected His mother with John by giving each to the
support of the other. Surely all true lovers have the same desire
to connect those they love. I have this desire for you, my love.

I am not suggesting that you move in with one of our children. As you would say, "Heaven forbid!" Independence is
healthy. I just encourage you to retain many loving, supporting
relationships, for knowing and loving creates us.

Yet, even as I was writing this section of my love-will, I
hesitated when you asked me about spending a weekend
with your brother. Remember how I joked about in-laws and
outlaws? Too late in life I am learning that dismissing people

before taking the time to know them is an insult. I especially regret destroying bridges rather than repairing or building them, for part of a lover's job description is that of bridge builder. At the very least, a lover shouldn't get in the way of the building. Perhaps I will have mended my ways and bridges will be stronger before you read this love-will. If not, I trust that you forgive my moods and selfishness.

Take comfort from our family and friends. They are so very important to balance the cold reality of death and separation. The funeral director and strangers may help for a few short days, but our families and friends are a continuing gift. They are our heritage, and they carry a promise and a vision of your future with them. Accept their comfort. I will always be connected with you in the memory and the reality of family and friends.

A Word About Family Pain

*Family life! The United Nations is child's play
compared to the tugs and splits and needs to
understand and forgive in any family.*

May Sarton

The family will gather within hours, but be gone again in a few days before they can be savoured. Because you are numbed by grief their visits may seem like a dream that you can't quite recall in the light of day.

"They could have stayed longer," you may say. But all of our families in turn have their own families and their own busy lives. Perhaps, too, they will detect your ambivalence – your need for them and your need to be alone. In any case, people only allot a few short days or perhaps just a single visit for funerals. Lack of time causes part of the stress of funerals and paying respects.

After experiencing our family at the funeral, you may well

wonder, "Where is the loving family?" Family pain is a reality that surfaces when families gather whatever the occasion. I am sure our family and my funeral will be no exception.

There are those who have some idea of "what should be done." They may help by taking charge and making decisions. But everything happens so quickly at funerals that often there isn't time to consult with others. Poor communication results in misunderstandings. People have different personalities and values and will be meeting under very stressful conditions. It is inevitable that you or others in our family won't like the way some things are done. That's life.

Family stress brings out the best and the worst in people. This is not a contradiction but simply a truthful comment on our human condition. It is understandable because suffering and compassion have the capacity to soften us until we are most human. We lower our defences. Friends can reach us more easily and healing can take place. But stress, tiredness, and emotions also make us less rational. The challenge of love is to have compassion for our suffering families without responding to the many symptoms of their pain. Their bitter tears, angry words, and sullen withdrawal – all symptoms of their hurt – are so visible. I pray that you may see beyond any of these symptoms and still take comfort.

Family and friends gather to share your grief and to comfort you by their presence. No one can take away your bitter cup. The most the loving can do is to share it. It isn't a matter of misery liking company or even sharing making the load lighter. We are healed by a community that shares our pain.

We acknowledge the hurt caused by others, but we forget that healing is the opposite of hurting. "That hurt," we say, but if we acknowledge kindness at all, we seldom say, "That healed." More likely we would say: "That felt good" or "That was considerate." But we are healed by people who are present, who care, and who listen. Acknowledge that healing is the opposite of hurting, and let our family and friends be present in your pain to heal you with their love.

I pray that you let any family disagreements pass, for the actual funeral arrangements or other business over which our family might quarrel are unimportant. Whatever their differences, my love, they will come to be with you because they love you. I pray that this focus helps you accept all their actions as loving. A lover sees others as imperfect lovers, each different, but loving as they are able.

Reflections for Your Memories of Me

Our memories are card indexes consulted
and then returned in disorder by authorities
whom we do not control.

Cyril Connolly

I will always be connected with you through memories, my love, for memories are our special heritage and our lasting bond. But, I am sure your memories now are bittersweet. You probably feel abandoned as you painfully sort through your memories alone. My desire is to be with you and to provide a loving perspective that may help you with your task. May love permeate all your memories and give you comfort.

You have inherited our lifetime of memories, but grief will make them seem like investments in a volatile stock market. Ups and downs can ruin market speculators who are only in for short-term gain. We were committed to the long term, where growth outweighed the losses. If you have hard memories that consume your thoughts, I hope that this longer perspective of our investment in each other gives you comfort.

May you fully accept your memories of our time together. They are gifts that we created together, but they are uniquely yours. You own them fully; they are not mine that I can alter them for you now. My memories of our time, too, are uniquely mine. They also cannot be given, only shared. Love never desires to steal or change another's memories. I will not try to talk you out of the honest feelings that they produce. My desire is merely to help you keep the reality of your memories intact.

Now even your happiest memories of me are touched by death. Know that I am with you as you accept my death in each memory. Let each memory die and have its resurrection. Memories will become less painful and more comforting. If they are too painful now, accept on faith that they will ultimately be reborn to become your friends.

The sharing of our separate halves of memories in life – our loaf – was like the breaking of the bread. It was the sharing of this loaf that fed our friendship. The lost sharing is the kneading and the leaven that any surviving spouse must mourn. Breaking the bread of our shared memories was easy, too. But sharing them now with another may be difficult – like having to explain the punch line of a private joke. You will grieve this loss. Even this love-will is static words upon the pages and not at all like our love-sustaining memories.

We built our memories together, but I leave the reality and the truth of them with you. Don't be concerned about the details of specific memories for they are unimportant now. Your memories will change with your emotions and as you are comforted. Merely keep the memories within the fabric of our whole life together and you will preserve their healthy truth.

A Comforting Thought
for Hurting Memories

There are no easy signposts, only a
lonely road
That each one travels with his
suffering.

Miriam Waddington

I cannot know your recent memories, or the pain I caused in them, for I am writing from our past. I do not know if you will read these words two or twenty years from now. My recent memories of which I can write may be dimly in your past. I can only pray for your sake that I will be attentive near the end of my allotted time, and that you will have loving memories of me. I pray that they do not ever lead you to deny that I love you, but only to accept that I was an imperfect lover.

Imperfect lover. Please ponder this phrase, for the noun captures the two great commandments to love God, and to love others like we do ourselves. Yet the adjective acknowledges the reality of a struggling humanity that often fails. I, like every lover, had to daily confess the failure of my calling. My failures affect those who are nearest me – those I love. It is natural for you to have equally strong memories of me loving you and hurting you. You could remember the hurt or the love and make me exclusively sinner or saint, but the truth is in neither extreme. I am just an imperfect lover. Remembering me as such may help you spiritually and mentally as you face all your memories, both pleasant and painful. It may help you avoid the temptation of repainting your memories as you think about our life together. I pray that this description also helps you to remember me as always loving you.

It Is Natural to Wonder Why

We also wonder "Why me?" or "Why did he die?" Looking for deeper answers to these unknowns is part of the quest of most grieving people.

Judy Tatelbaum

Great minds have wrestled with the "why" of death. I will not attempt their logical arguments, for their best "because" offers little comfort for a grieving lover.

Yet, "why" is an important part of grief. It is important to you also, so I cannot let it pass. Loving spouses acknowledge such questions even though they have no answers, for true lovers do not ignore hurts even if they cannot change them. They have learned that others need their presence in their pain more than they need answers. And so, my love, I want you to know that I accept your "why," and that I am with you in your questioning. I hope my presence provides some comfort.

Perhaps this presence is like communion because in it a

lover both accepts another's pain – gives himself to suffer with the other – and becomes a part of their mysterious healing. But it is also like the miracle of the loaves and fishes for lovers feel so inadequate when faced with another's pain that they must give themselves in faith and pray for the miracle that will help fill the other's need.

Perhaps we are like children when we question death. They go through a normal stage of questioning as we do in grief. For every answer to their endless questions, they merely repeat "But why?" Our children do not argue just to test our patience, although they often do. Sometimes their questions represent curiosity meeting answers beyond their comprehension. But usually not, because they do it most often when they are out of sorts and when our answers are quite simple. Most often their questioning is just a protest of disagreeable reasons.

Questioning death is childlike, because whatever answers we find will always be incomprehensible or disagreeable to us. But, the answers are incomprehensible precisely because they are shrouded in the Mystery that is God. If we accept that "why" touches part of Mystery, then faith becomes our comforting ally. This faith comforts us by assuring us of an ultimate meaning even though it is beyond us. This faith also comforts us because our terrible "why" must connect us with the beautiful why of our lives. The Mystery of death is part of the same Mystery of love and joy we felt when we held our first-born child, when we walked in peace through a mountain meadow, or when overcome with joy by an unexpected kindness. I pray that the "why" of my death is balanced by the why of beauty, the why of our love, and the why of creation in our children. But we are like our young children who questioned why we sent them to bed, without also questioning why we always read a bedtime story and kissed them goodnight. The balance comes later.

Although death is disagreeable, there is comfort in knowing that it is inevitable and natural. Eternal life is a mystery. And yet, Jesus both grieved and died. In His why of grief, He cried and called Lazarus to life, and in the passion of death, He questioned why he was forsaken. Whatever the answers to death and grief, they do not separate us either from nature or from our God.

Your questioning stage will pass as it does for children, and not because of new answers, but because of a growing acceptance of old ones. The "why" of grief is mostly one of denial. When it fades away, this marks the initial step of acceptance. Accept the dual comforts: This stage of grief is natural and it will pass.

Questioning can be healthy, only temper it with love. For children, questioning ultimately defines them. It shapes them into healthy, productive adults or else stagnates them in rebellion. It is love that tips the balance in favour of their growth, for love prevents them from becoming hard and bitter. Love will also do the same for you, my love. May your "why" be productive, and may it slowly turn the "why" that questions life into the "why not" that lets life gently question you and lead you onward.

In the midst of your "why," a lover would offer one caution: Don't blame it on God. That would be the same dead end as children blaming their parents. It kills or stunts them. Yet, if you do blame God, take comfort, for this will pass. Take comfort, too, that God tolerates our anger just as good parents tolerate this emotion in their children. God succeeds where we might fail; an honest lament can be a prayer.

I hope you feel me lovingly with you. I wanted to conclude with a special comfort for your questioning, but only two words keep popping into mind: Mystery and freedom. I tried to get a hold on these words but the Mystery is beyond me. And freedom shocked me for my image was of laughter and I feared that this image would not be helpful. Yet laughter is natural as death is natural. And so, I give you Mystery and the freedom to laugh, but also the freedom to weep as Jesus wept for Lazarus. I also leave you the paradoxical Mystery that gives equal comfort both from your laughter and your tears.

Comfort Will Come

Blessed are they that mourn
for they shall be comforted.

Matthew 5:5

I just finished reading *A Severe Mercy* and I imagine that, like for Sheldon Vanauken in his grief, God will also seem more distant to you when I am gone. That is the way of grief. Perhaps when you most need to feel God's presence, there is comfort in remembering the promise in the Beatitude.

Accept on faith, my love, that God is a constant abyss of love and compassion that is always there for us whatever our feelings. Your experience of desolation is a common and an expected one because grief turns us inward to focus on our pain. This is normal even though it is the opposite to turning outward, to loving, and to giving, which make us more receptive to God's comfort. Your days of desolation will pass. In the meantime, take your ultimate comfort on faith.

But remember the Beatitude inseparably links the comfort with the mourning. Doctors also say that mourning is necessary and that your future health will depend on how completely you have grieved. Neither God nor doctors say that you will be comforted and healed without having fully grieved your loss. So then, Oh God, where is Your comfort? It's only in accepting the pain of grief and in mourning. Grief is not meant to be a fixed and crippling state, but action – a process.

You can't get around grief, and it would be crippling to wallow in it and wait for comfort. You have to go through it. Mourning is not the pain, but rather, grief in action as you plod through. Endure. There is comfort on the other side. This is the full promise of the Beatitude. Take comfort in it.

The expression of love changes. What was yesterday's love and commitment become today's mourning, and promises to be tomorrow's comforting. Perhaps it helps to see your mourning as the reflection of our love – just love with a different face. Later you will be comforted and you will be able to comfort others. Being predisposed to mourn and to comfort reflect the same divine love, therefore, you are blessed. Be patient, my love.

Our fall from a close love relationship with God was catastrophic. Scientists do not have the instruments to measure the reverberations in our hearts from this event because the tool needed is prayer, and that has been the specialty of poets and lovers. Nonetheless, the reverberations are in all hearts as a longing for a love that cannot be fully satisfied in this world. Saint Augustine says, "Thou hast made us for Thyself, Oh Lord and our hearts are restless until they rest in Thee." Even an agnostic falls in love with love itself, and mourns a lost love in addition to the lost lover. Your mourning goes beyond our love and is a cry of longing from your restless heart. Such mourning is blessed because it is of God and is grounded in hope. This also is a meaning of the Beatitude.

I seldom mention sympathy but I assure you that I do not lack it. Sympathy is such an easily misunderstood word that I tried to avoid it. The first meaning of sympathy that comes to my mind is pity. Understanding, compassion, and empathy are alternative words that steer clear of the negative quagmire of self-pity – "the private pity party," as we used to say. Know that my words are of understanding, compassion, and empathy, but you do not need pity from your friends or from me either. What we all need is love.

These words may seem harsh, but please accept that they are equally of love – a pep talk should you need it. The dance of life invites you to accept my death. It urges you to force yourself to face all the places in your life and in your heart where I am now absent and to love by mourning and moving on. Although the dance is tiring and painful, it is not in vain because when you are through you will find your comfort.

Hope Even in Your Darkest Days

Hope is faith holding out its hands in the dark.

George Iles

I am writing this section after a crab session at work. I came home thinking there should be a warning sign in the coffee room. "Danger! Coffee breaks in these premises can be damaging to your mental and spiritual health!" I'm aware how negative and pessimistic people drag us down, whereas optimistic, loving people restore us and predispose us to hope. Do you remember the good laugh we shared about a Peanuts cartoon? Snoopy knocks on Lucy's door and kisses her when she opens the door. Snoopy walks away thinking, "That's the way to break up a crab-in."

You have broken up a lot of my crab-ins. I thank you for the your large part in keeping a positive, optimistic, and hopeful environment in our home. My desire is to do the same for you in your grief. I ask you to remember love and to keep an attitude of love with family and friends. Force yourself to be involved with people in a positive way even if you have to pretend. I believe love not only breaks up crab-ins, but also lessens grief.

Grief is like depression in the way it sucks away your future and leaves you feeling hopeless. "What can I do with all my pain and will it ever stop? What about my dreams? What does the future hold for me? Will I ever really enjoy doing anything again? Will I always feel empty and alone? What is the purpose of my life? Will I ever laugh and feel whole again?"

I want, like any lover, to counter your hopelessness with hope. You wonder if your life will ever be normal again, and I assure you that you won't always feel this way. You have to go through grief, but it will pass if you persevere and comfort will follow like the sun after a winter storm. That is your ray of hope. Continue to force yourself to do things now even when you don't feel like it. You won't always have to pretend and push yourself to do things. Gradually pleasure will come. Hope will return and it will bring a new future.

Hope is a virtue. It's a divine gift that wells up from the spirit within. But lovers know that love nurtures hope, and that is why I left you my love-will. I hope that it restores some of the purpose that grief has sucked away. The loss of hope is what makes grief so terrible. But believe, my love, that way off there is a faint light at the end of the tunnel. That light is hope. Believe that despair will pass and something new will come of your life. Trust it, pray for it, and nurture it. It will happen.

Dark questions will naturally come to you in sleepless nights for these questions are part of the hopelessness of grief. Sometimes you will question whether our relationship meant anything at all. This love-will is especially for those times. I pray it is apparent on every page that our relationship was meaningful. Read my love-will as you need for your assurance that the past was both real and worthwhile, as you are, too, my love. Don't let grief suck the meaning out of you or your past.

"Whatever our relationship, it's all gone," you may lament. Not really, for you carry it with you. It's part of the strength of who you are now. You climbed mountains and crossed dark valleys in the past. Let the past give you faith in yourself and let this give you cause to hope.

Hope is not like our expectations. Lovers strive to limit their expectations, for expectations are specific and often negative because they make demands of others or else disappoint us when they are not realized. Expectations often harden and get chiselled in stone. They are like your expectation that I not leave my dirty socks on the floor when I slip into bed. Did I make you smile? Hope doesn't expect something specific. It is more of a trust that something will happen and that our life will unfold in a meaningful way. Hope is the prayer of a lover's soul.

The past is so painful now because of death, but this pain will gradually pass and I will rest more gently on your mind. Lovers believe in the eternal quality of love. Your hope for a peaceful, lingering connection with me will be realized. I will always be with you in some different and beautiful way. This hope of our faith can make grief more bearable. On dark and gloomy days, we know the sun is no less real and know that it will shine tomorrow. And in our better moments we believe in love that always shines and is more than just the two of us. This love grounds our faith. It will always shine and is our hope. I pray that this aspect of love is apparent throughout my love-will.

My main desire in all my words is to linger with you. I want to reaffirm the reality of love for to feel love is to hope. My prayer for you is hope in the rubble of broken expectations. My hope for you is warm as an unexpected kiss. It's a desire that longing take root in a hope that warms and sustains you. All my love-will speaks of love and is of hope for a love-will is just a prayer, as hope is but a prayer and the exhortation of the soul.

Perhaps You Blame Me for Dying

Our imaginations toy with the idea that "if he had loved me, he would not have died."

Judy Tatelbaum

Most of the time we deny that we are frail, finite, and mortal. But it's a miracle we survive so long. Certainly, death is to be expected and blame for it is seldom rational. Although we know death is beyond our control, the grieving usually blame the dead or themselves.

Likely I will have no choice in the matter and neither will you. Aside from taking reasonable care of my health and avoiding accidents, I can do nothing because death comes without our beckoning. But logic will be of little value when you face the task of accepting my death so I will try again and speak to your heart.

I am truly sorry if you ever feel that I have deserted you.

Whatever the circumstances of my death, I would never wish to leave you. Our Maker designed us to hang onto life and to fight to the end, as I am sure I will do. Biologists assure us that self-preservation is the strongest of all human drives. But, perhaps, a look of peacefulness will come over my face in death to belie me. If so, it is part of the mystery of death. Let me simply say that I would not embrace death. This phrase is just one of many indications that we view death incorrectly. The inevitable is seldom embraced. Resignation is closer, but the mystery is acceptance because that will be the origin of peace, both for me in death and for you in life.

This explanation won't surprise you, but you may need to be gently reminded of it in your grief. Hints of this truth are all around us. For instance, consider people who live in bitterness because they cannot accept some wrong done to them in the past, or consider some people in our hospitals who can't even accept themselves. Their prognosis is poor until they accept themselves or their particular situation. Grief is not different; death must be accepted to be completed in peace.

Relativity is a great unifying theory that makes sense of many diverse and seemingly unrelated facts in science, mathematics and physics. Similarly, acceptance is the great unifying principle for personal peace. It draws together experiences and truisms from religion and psychology, as well as from personal lives and deaths.

What can I say to comfort you? Ultimately words fail me. I am like your friends who now struggle for words to speak and then generally end up saying something inappropriate or remaining silent. I do not want to leave you. I will not desert you, but I may be called to take the low road while you are left to the high road. I will disappear from the sphere of your senses but I won't have passed into nothingness. In some way, I will still be, for that is the mystery of our faith. I ask you to draw upon this mystery. If my words are inadequate, please consider me standing beside you with a hand on your shoulder.

Have the Courage to Choose

Courage is the affirmative choice,
not a choice because "I can do no other . . . "

Rollo May

I have been reflecting on my visit to the cemetery where my father is buried. His name was on the left side of his tombstone and below were the dates of his birth and death – his life reduced and captured in his name and allotted time. But still more unsettling was my mother's name and her year of birth on the right side of the stone, for she is still living, yet her epitaph, too, was complete except for the final chiselled date.

Other dual stones surrounded me; each announced a spouse awaiting death. My memory of that visit is not of the dead and buried like my father, but of the awaited death of others like my mother. Announced. Pending yet lingering. Suspended in a disturbing social death. Statistics show that too many widows and widowers die within months of their mates. The truth is not the idealization of lovers dying together but a loss of their will to live. Perhaps the incomplete markers echo this: the living trained in the school of life and love with no will to live. I am saddened by any possibility that you fit this image of emptiness and awaited death.

What sobering imagery to a parting lover for love itself would be for naught – wasted – if it left only emptiness. If so little were created that it not only died but also killed! However, love does not end up killing when it is gone. Human love, however feeble, is part of the life-giving mystery of love. There is no death from love except in turning away and withdrawing into a shrinking, private waiting. Love turned in – collapsing upon itself – is an antithesis to the omnipresent and omnipotent love of God.

By the time you read this, you may have planned for your own death by erecting a dual marker on my grave. If so, this reflection on choices must sound like a contradiction of the freedom I emphasized in making funeral arrangements. Remember, my love, these are merely my impressions, not yours. Instead of death such a marker may announce your healthy acceptance of the reality of death or a thoughtfulness toward our children in making final arrangements. Perhaps the tombstone yells out that here is death, but you live on till the final date and period are set. The same stone can give impressions of death or of life. The stones themselves are not important, only the way we view them, which brings me to my point. We have a choice in our view of life and we can choose to live.

I pray that you accept my death as chiselled in stone, yet see your own life incomplete, unbracketed, unbounded, unrestricted: a line continuing indefinitely into the future. Live in the fullest meaning of life. Accept that love changes its expression, yet we must continually love – yes, even as you experience my death. Also accept the rebirth of love in your relationships with others for such is the unending process of life and our calling as lovers.

I pray that you may have the conviction to continue to be a lover, for there is turmoil and pain in any relationship. It's a truth of life. In your grief you can see the pain more clearly and count the cost. But you still must choose, for life is choosing – not choosing is awaiting death.

I write about choices because the "getting by" and waiting of grief is not enough. On the outside, detached and uninvolved, you may see only struggles and strife. Wade into life again to join the full struggle and, even if nothing changes, you are a lover and that attitude will make a difference. It's the echo of the invitation to pain, "Take up your cross and follow me" and the paradox of love, "My yoke is light."

May you ever choose life and be comforted.

About Cleaning My Closets

I went through her things like a storm —
a sorrowing storm —
giving to friends what she had told me to give them.

Sheldon Vanauken

We tried again this week to clean up our storage areas, but without too much success. We joked about having to be in the right mood. By the right mood, we meant a giveaway mood instead of our usual pack-rat mood. I think the right mood has largely escaped us for our boxes of stuff "that one day we might want" have stuck to us like a wad of bubble gum. I imagine when I am gone you will find boxes that we never unpacked from our last move. It's what I call the dung beetle view of life. Dung beetles lay their eggs in balls of dung and spend most of their lives fashioning the balls to their liking and struggling to roll them along. People also spend a lifetime fashioning their dung balls which they protect and roll with them till they die.

Some even think there is a prize for how big a ball they can shape and how far they can roll it. Did I raise a smile?

Trimming the ball, my dear, will be more difficult than when we faced our closets together. I hope that you find your "right mood" – that you find a balance between retaining your history and making space for new growth. There is nothing in the closets that I want you either to keep or to discard for death cures dung beetle lives. When you read this love-will, my want will be gone and my desire is only your well-being.

Closets may seem trivial, my love, but they are the repositories for all the mementos of our past. Each of them, whether a treasure or a forgotten piece of junk, lays waiting for you with its full emotional story. This truth is why dealing with our closets will mark a milestone in your grief. I will share some thoughts and feelings as I envision you packing my belongings. If some of my visions are unreal to you, as I am sure they will be, then simply ignore them. For the real ones, I pray that I touch them with a comforting love. I pray that you feel my understanding and support.

I suspect our closets will create an urgency and some pressure from our friends. I can imagine their hints. "I'm free on Tuesday if you need help sorting his things." You may feel that they are not very subtle in telling you to get on with your life. You're right, but their emotions are complicated, too. Everyone who loves you empathizes and suffers with you for this is what it means to be united in the spirit of all love. Doing jobs for you, or even asking to, is important to our friends.

There is another reason for the concern about my belongings. Unfortunately, most of our friends have heard of someone who never accepted a loved one's death. Although such denial is unusual beyond the initial stages of grieving, our friends may think it is a common problem. To state their fear bluntly, my love, they fear that you will create a museum of my personal effects instead of accepting my death and moving on with your life. But you may want comforting reminders of my presence. I would not worry about this difference. I am confident that you will find your balance in your own time.

People approach life with such tremendous urgency – like we do now in our marriage. It seems normal and we seldom question even the worst clichés about urgency: Take charge. Get on with it. Onward and upward. Take the fast lane. But grief is low gear, slow motion, and even a fight with lethargy. Please take some comfort from your slower pace even though our society is somewhat intolerant of life in the slow lane. At a time when you struggle for new connectedness, even your sense of time may separate you from your friends. Take comfort in knowing that your slower pace is normal and that it will pass.

Our friends may also see that my belongings sometimes distress you. They naturally assume that if they were disposed of you would be upset less often and would be improving. They do not realize that their simplistic perception completely misses the point, which is your feelings and needs. It is you who must work through your grief. You may well need some of my things and the feelings they elicit to help you for a while. Our friends are concerned about your state, whereas your state is less important to you than the process of your grieving.

Love, fear, concern, and comfort will be some of the emotions of your volunteer closet-cleaners. My desire is to stand beside you as I used to do when we went sightseeing. We would point things out to each other, and see and enjoy more than if we were alone. Now I merely point out the humanness and genuine love of our friends so you do not miss their comfort. I pray that I have pointed out something of beauty to be shared in your bleak and weathered landscape. May you always see me as standing with you and may this comfort you. See, too, the love and concern of our friends, and take comfort in them as you do what you have to do. I am ever proud of you.

Frustration and Anger Are Normal

We want people to feel with us more than to
act for us.

George Eliot

When I last wrote, I envisioned friends empathizing and offering to help clean our closets. I want to share more about that because you may be surprised by feelings of frustration and anger. You may feel that some friends are insensitive to your feelings and needs when they try to help you. At times this is likely, as few people are trained to deal with emotions, and in the school of life, we all learn too little too late.

You may feel that they treat you like a child. Although I suspect most of our friends will be marvellous, some seem compelled to make decisions for vulnerable people. Unfortunately, they easily succumb to temptation and place the elderly, the physically challenged, and the grieving into a helpless class with the very young. Without thinking, they take charge and make decisions. This is especially true of those who have not learned to listen well or to empathize without feeling compelled to solve problems.

You won't intend to offend anyone, least of all good friends, but they may get in your space and time for grieving. Annoyance or even flashes of anger may confuse you. You may wonder about your anger because it will seem to be about insignificant things like closets. I suspect such anger is about control. As you struggle to take charge of your life, some of our family and friends may seem ready to take charge of it for you. You have always been in charge of your life. Help from friends in the past has not been a threat to your control, but your organized life and your confidence have been badly damaged. Take comfort from understanding your anger and knowing that it is natural to feel conflicting emotions. I have confidence in you. Your frustration will pass and you will feel in control again.

Let Grief Pass

> *. . . shed tears over a dead man . . . bury his body*
> *with due ceremonial . . . observe the mourning the*
> *dead man deserves, one day, or two to avoid*
> *comment, and then be comforted in your*
> *sorrow . . . Let grief end with the funeral . . .*
>
> **Ecclesiastics 38:16–19**

I have been reflecting on this advice on grief. The words may seem harsh so I am writing to assure you that they are what any lover might write for a grieving spouse. They are not the order of a general: I command you, BE COMFORTED. They are simply the gentle urging of the spirit to allow yourself to be comforted – to accept that grief is not an end in itself. Grief is neither a virtue to be cultivated nor a treasure to be locked up and savoured in your heart.

In my mind's eye I see your moments of comfort – moments of peaceful solitude amid your loneliness, beauty amid your desolation. Little things noticed: the warmth of the sun on your body, sounds of children laughing at play, the trees whispering and shimmering in the breeze. I easily imagine you absorbing many sensations from the good life around you. You may fill with a joy of life but then a cloud of doubt darkens your spirits: "How can I feel so good when he is gone? Have I become so cold and unloving that even grief will not be my companion?"

What a quandary. Grief is not a companion to travel with you for life. Yet even so a good friend will let you grow and give you space for new friends. We often wonder about ourselves when a companion leaves us, even if we are better off. Is it my fault that the friend is leaving? Have I offended? Or, perhaps the friend has discovered what I'm really like. If grief is like a friend, don't second-guess yourself when it departs.

Once you probably felt your grief would never end, but now you may question when it is absent. You may feel that if you love me my death should continue to cause great pain. Yet at times there is none and the absence may surprise and even shock you. My labour of love is to show you that the niggling inclination to feel miserable, although natural, comes from a darker mixture of emotions, for love urges you to be comforted.

What would love say about any feelings of guilt? Guilt is the hand that steals your comfort. It clutches close to the chest and will not surrender, whereas love is the open, outstretched hand that always gives comfort. Recognize the sporadic nature of grief and that hanging onto grief does not show stronger love for me, only that your promised gift of comfort has been stolen by guilt or other negative feelings.

Perhaps you think that your feelings should be consistent. Not so, my love, for happy moments are normal in the midst of even the first painful periods of grief, for grief is more like protracted labour pains than a dull, continuous toothache. Pangs of grief are sharp, and they don't become less painful. They simply change in frequency. This analogy is apropos, too, because new life comes from labour pains as it also comes from your pangs of grief.

The traditional black clothes and mournful expressions of the past can easily come to mind when we think of grief. These memories make it easier to accept the assumption that grief should be consistently dark and sorrowful. Love urges you to reconsider this assumption. Mourning is a reevaluation and an adjusting to an absence. It is the process of healing and doesn't have to be continually painful. It may well involve new activities that are challenging and exciting. If so, accept this excitement of life as part of your mourning. Your joy and laughter will show you are free and left with a greater capacity to love life – a legacy. Celebrate your lifted spirits.

In love I urge you. Please don't mourn your loss of grief when it is absent. Don't attempt to recapture it in the recesses of your heart. Let grief take its course for it cannot be forced. It is just another emotion that comes and goes beyond our control. You can no more hold on to moments of grief then we could our moments of contentment. Let me die in your grief and be reborn in your joy of life.

It Is All Right to Do Well Without Me

Capability is a virtue.

Anonymous

You may remember my little quirk of saying, "You done good!" Poor grammar aside, those three words are difficult for me to improve upon. Anyway, who cares about grammar when the words provide a good stroke of validation? Perhaps I hide behind the poor grammar and that makes the compliment easier to give. Why do we find it so hard to say the things that mean so much to others? No wonder we leave so much unfinished business when we die.

I am sure you are doing well. It is normal during grief to feel overwhelmed with periods of helplessness and inactivity. These periods will pass. When they do, you may have the illogical feeling of "I'm doing too well without him," for it easily sneaks into honest grief. The idea that one should show grief by being helpless is mistaken. Grief that inactivates does not show that a dead lover is better mourned. It has shades of the false thinking that I shared about my funeral – that mourning is something you do for me rather than for yourself. Grief is to heal you, my love, not to further wound you.

You are very capable, my love. I have every confidence that you will move on in your life with good decisions. Know this in your heart and let this knowledge comfort you. Your capability is a virtue. Any lover would be remiss if he did not remind his beloved of this truth. Love delights in all virtue, as I rejoice in your capability. Don't let grief undermine your capabilities.

When You Talk to Me

*Gracie died in 1964, and I still go to Forest Lawn
cemetery once a month to see her. I stand in front of
her marble monument and tell her everything that's
going on in my life. I don't know if she hears me,
but I know that after speaking to her, I feel better.*

George Burns

I remember one special occasion when we came home early
from an evening out together. Our lovemaking was long and
satisfying, and seemed to flow naturally from our evening.
Later as we rested warmly in each other's arms, you whispered
for me to share my prayer with you. In fact, I often pray for
you, as I am sure you do for me, but how did you know I was
thanking God for the love He gives me in you? You may
remember that a long silence followed. In spite of your natural
request, I could not immediately recover from my feeling of
exposure. We eventually whispered our prayer in the darkness
of our bed. I want to thank you for that special evening and the
many more we shared.

As I reflect, it's curious how we talk about most things, including sex, but were usually too self-conscious and felt too naked to share our personal prayers. When the spirit of love filled us, we usually prayed separately in thanksgiving, and when we quarrelled, we also prayed but separately in repentance. What a pity that the armour of lovers against the world is so strong that it also shields their souls from each other by muffling the words of their spirits.

I imagine that one day in your grief you will begin to talk to me like George Burns did to Gracie for it's natural and most lovers eventually do. You may even find yourself praying to me. Such a prayer may flow out of our love and need, like our shared prayer of thanksgiving. In fact, even agnostics reach a period in their grief when they have a quiet chat with their dead lover. They complete unfinished business, and talk about their plans as they put their lives back together. It seems a natural part of making a final good-bye, and so it is.

I am only guessing, but you may find in praying that you mingle talking to God with talking to me. Your prayer may start simply with reflections about us and our relationship. Later you may pour out your struggle and ask for help. You may even tell me what it feels like to be deserted when you had so much of your life and happiness invested in our relationship. You may recall our time together just before my death and any regretted words or actions. You may ask for help in understanding, accepting and forgiving for these are all parts of a lover's prayer. Whatever comes from your needs, my prayer is that it feels as right as the prayer we shared from our marital bed and that it gives you comfort.

I share my reflections on a lover's prayer because we are so one-dimensional in our society that we cannot comprehend the idea of an omnipresent God. It is interesting that we see our sin against each other as also against God, as it rightly is. It follows though, since God is in and of all things, that all our prayers rise to God. This is especially true since the spirit of God within us calls us to prayer in the first place. However, if you find yourself praying to me and feel uncomfortable, just call it a little chat. My desire is just that you be free and that you accept this comfort.

Our faith is shaken when a loved one dies and this can cripple our prayer. Chatting with our deceased one is effective because it enables our souls to cry out in prayer even when we feel distant from God.

"She simply worships him," we say. No wonder we are confused by a lover's prayer. But our use is merely an overstatement, like saying that we love ice cream. Life would be less confusing if we were more careful with our words, and learned again to like things, to love people, and to worship God. But perhaps the distinction between prayer and worship is too trivial to worry about for we love each other best when we see

God in each other – when life is reverent, and the other is a holy temple.

Some people end up not forgiving God, and some not forgiving their departed spouse or themselves. These are reactions to the same hurts that heal from honest prayer. Remember our time together and that we cared enough about our relationship to be honest with each other and our feelings. We didn't walk away. We exchanged words, sometimes in passion, but our relationship endured. And so it is in all our relationships with God and each other. So pray with anger, tears and as much emotion as you want. Know that I rejoice that your relationship with God and your memories of me are not lost in a morass of retained grievances accompanied by silence in your heart. Comfort will come.

Time is God's gift for us because we cannot understand our grief, accept love, or heal all at once. Think of time as God's way of administering small doses of love, healing, and mercy as we are able to accept them. The grieving often cry out to God, but are so centred in their grief that even the first dose of love and mercy is too much for them to accept. It is like trying to describe the beauty of a mountain scene to someone who is blind or, more appropriate still, like trying to give to someone who will not accept.

You have heard, "He is with God now." This cliché is too simple, and yet, what more can I say? It is not for us to understand death, but in not understanding it we must not misinter-pret it. The resurrection means that death is not a godless void. God is with us always. Always! Even in death. When all else has changed, our omnipresent God is the constant and prayer is what binds us to God and to each other, living and dead.

Accept comfort from praying to me as you like, for it will bring you closer to recovery and worship. Our love truly is a gift. And a prayer to a dead lover is special, for it is of the spir-it, and it's yours – your prayer to whisper or to scream. Know that the spirit is within the source of the whisper or the scream, and Yahweh hears it. Believe that I am always with you in love and that I also pray for you. Also believe that lovers hear all prayers. I will be a better listener than I am now as I write and I will never interrupt!

May My Love Set You Free

Perhaps love is the process of my leading you
gently back to yourself. Not to whom I want
you to be, but to who you are.

Leo. F. Buscaglia

Sometimes as I write, I catch myself repeating sentiments that I have already expressed and I think that I should scratch out the repeated phrases and start again – that I should express thoughts once and be done with them. But that is my brain speaking. The heart of a lover repeats its message like a broken record: I love you. The news is echoed in words and actions a dozen times a day. Once would be enough to inform, but lovers know that their words must also feed the spirit. So I may repeat sentiments in my love-will in response to different situations. My desire is to linger with thoughts and words that feed your spirit. Yet, if you are full, put my love-will aside. All it says over and over again in different ways is that I love you, and that I pray for your re-creation.

The spirit of love never asked me to solve your problems – not as your husband, nor now in this love-will. Loving doesn't mean taking charge and doing for others what they can do for themselves for that is crippling. Nor does love mean providing solutions for even the best intended are polluted with control. Loving others is the opposite of controlling them. I have come to see that to love you I must let go of all my control, join you in the midst of your uncertainty, stand with you and encourage you, but give you freedom to share your struggle and search for your path.

I struggled all my life to give up controlling you. I suppose death has succeeded where I failed. I pray that I am successful in loving you without control in this love-will, for my desire is to love you perfectly. Love demands no less of me than that I let you be the person you are meant to be. But even this statement falls short, for "let" implies that I am still in control and giving my permission. Please accept that I do not intend any control, but if it has crept in, as I am sure it has, know that when you read this I will be dead. Remember my opening disclaimer. Disregard anything that appears to be controlling.

Talking About Me

In the telling of their stories, strangers befriend
not only their host but also their past.

Henri Nouwen

Like all North Americans, you will be handicapped in working
through your grief because people are reluctant to talk about
the dead. Merely mentioning my name may evoke a strange
mixture of embarrassment and sympathy. I empathize with
you. It is not as easy to mourn in our society as in others. I have
heard that in some countries the whole family gets together
three months, six months, and one year after a death to talk
about the deceased and to share feelings. What a support
group, and what healing must be possible in such gatherings!

The closer our relationship in marriage and the better our
communication, the more you will miss our sharing. No matter
how I try, I know that these words cannot substitute for our

sharing. I hope they provide some comfort, but the loss of our talking is best mourned by talking to others.

You will probably tell our friends the details of my death. It seems a natural thing to do and repeating the story will help convince you that it is true. Later, speaking about emotions and our relationship will help you to accept them and will help you keep them real. I pray that you find someone who can really listen without offering unwanted advice, for someone special to talk to will be very important to you in your grief.

There is comfort in accepting complete freedom to mourn and talk about me. Open sharing will help you accept me as I was and will help you keep me more gently in your thoughts. If you accept that mourning is indeed for the living, and you feel this truth in the depths of your heart, then there is a new freedom to talk and mourn by sharing your feelings completely. Please accept this freedom as a gift of love and may your talking help to heal you.

You cannot be disloyal after I am dead. We were loyal to each other in our marriage and were careful about the information and feelings that we shared with others, but that time is past. You do not need permission now to talk about our relationship and share personal things about me. However, if you feel a need for my permission, be assured, my love, that you have it.

Recalling Our Quarrels

The kindest and the happiest pair
Will find occasion to forbear,
And something ev'ry day they live
To pity and, perhaps, forgive.

William Cowper

We sometimes quarrel about who and what is right or wrong. It would be nice to say that our quarrels are always positive. Sometimes they are, but often they just result from moments of ill disposition or strong will. Such quarrels were our little deaths when we rehearsed words in silence or else dumped them upon each other with too little regard. Yet our relationship survived these deaths for forgiving was its resurrection. I pray now that as you remember these deaths you also remember our resurrections.

Resolving differences with me is not always easy. If I had addressed your feelings and our differences more consistently along the way, they would not have built to the exploding point as they sometimes did. Probably now you regret some quarrels, and especially any recent ones that we may not have resolved before I died, for such regrets are normal in grief. Normal conflicts, though, are not necessarily bad – simply healthy opportunities for resolving differences and for growth. They are harmful only when not dealt with and then forgotten. Our marriage endured because we chose to resolve our differences. We loved each other enough to quarrel; for that I thank you.

I want to focus on any unresolved quarrels, for they may be the all-important ones to you as you read my love-will. Remember that our relationship is dynamic – a kaleidoscope of changing scenes. But my death will stop the action with final frames frozen on each screen of your memory. Some frames will undoubtedly be of conflict, for we are human. However trivial the conflict, your final frames from uncompleted scenes may be so vivid in your grief that any conflict in them will seem to represent the reality of our whole relationship. If this is the case for you, my love, believe that the resolution and growth would have occurred in those same scenes in future frames that were cut short by death. This is the faith of lovers. There would have been a resurrection. One cannot judge a motion picture by a single frame or the truth of a relationship except in its entirety.

In your grief, I see you travelling a narrow road with a precipice on either side. On the right is idealization, and if you should fall off that cliff you would make me perfect in your memories but I would become only a fantasy that would eventually get in the way of your healing. On the left is an abyss of continuing turmoil, and should you fall off that cliff you would not progress beyond the memories of arguments and anger that are a part of every marriage. And so I have acknowledged our quarrels and I ask you to do the same. I pray that you are able to keep me a whole person in your memories – neither saint nor scoundrel. After I am dead, the quarrels won't matter to me, but accepting them may be important for your future comfort and that is my desire for you.

Perhaps the abyss on your left frightens you toward idealization. You fear that you will not be able to keep your memories of love, and that warmth and comfort will be poisoned. Then, you fear, my death will be complete and I will truly be gone for ever. But you will also lose me if you make me something that I was not in life.

Or, perhaps, you are unable to speak or even think ill of the dead. You feel your mourning is for me and that your path of grief near the left precipice is somehow unacceptable. Remember, though, that love desires honesty from you and nothing more. Have faith that honesty will see you safely along your path to comfort wherever it should lead you. Remember, too, that love is unifying. Loving memories of me will not be poisoned by the honesty of your love.

Be assured, my love, that our quarrels were simply a normal part of our resolution of conflict. Yet if we were to be reunited tomorrow I would still be me, with all my quirks, and you would still be you. Nothing would have changed. Occasionally we would still quarrel, yet our love would endure.

Our marriage would have been dull without our differences. Thank you for the fire that shaped our marriage. Thank you for being a sensitive person who understood my feelings much better than I understood yours. Please forgive me for my poor understanding of you. Forgive me also for all the times that I provoked quarrels by being stubborn, blind, and insensitive to your feelings. Thank you, too, for helping me, sometimes even painfully stretching me through our quarrels, to be a bit more attuned to your feelings.

As in life, so in death. Please forgive me any pain I may cause you, and, as always, be assured of my forgiveness and my love.

Regrets: If Only . . .

The Moving Finger writes; and, having writ,
Moves on; nor all your Piety nor Wit
Shall lure it back to cancel half a Line
Nor all thy Tears wash out a Word of it.

The Rubáiyát of Omar Khayyám

After our friend, Louise, left the other night, I realized how plagued she is with regrets. She repeatedly said "if only." I began to wonder if you might go through a similar period of regret and what I could say in my love-will to comfort you.

I suspect there are always regrets when a loved one dies. Your "if only" feelings are normal and will often be beyond your control, but they can become a fantasy in grief and build castles out of what might have been. They imply living happily ever after rather than just taking a different fork in the road and going down an equally uncertain path.

While at first your "if only's" may come simply from your desire and be like a prayer of longing, they get easily out of hand. When "if only" loses touch with the reality of life it becomes a cruel game. A game not because any feelings of self-reproach are trivial, but because grief becomes an opponent that attacks you. It's love that comforts those that mourn, and there is no love in a cruel attack.

In love I ask you to reflect upon any feelings of regret. Feelings are not always rational. When "if only" fills your heart, I encourage you to think "then what?" This may seem like thinking up excuses, but the object is not to rationalize away but to find the truth. It would be uncharitable not to test your feelings, for grief often distorts responsibility. The commandment to love others as we do ourselves does not mean that we should heap blame and guilt upon ourselves. No one needs permission to examine their regrets. If upon examination you find a real basis for your regrets, know that I forgive you. If you find no real basis for them, accept your humanness and the reality of the situation.

Louise played the "if only" game so often in her grief it was like playing chess with many opening moves and each of these creating dozens more: "If only I had taken him to the hospital faster. If only I had encouraged him to exercise more. If only I had watched his diet. If only I had mowed the lawn for him. If only I had insisted on a medical check-up. If only . . . "

She knew all the moves by heart. She had trouble getting beyond the "if" of her feelings because she did not think "then what?" If she had tried to get him to the hospital faster, then she may have injured herself or others in the process and he still would have died. His heart attack was massive, which means then that it never was a question of time. But, then perhaps the doctors would have had time to hook him up to life support. He hated hospitals and feared becoming a vegetable connected to machines. So, then she may have added to his suffering.

Her "if only's" suggest that she should have spent years nagging him about his lack of exercise and overeating because these bad habits might kill him. But her nagging would have killed part of him long before. He was an adult and responsible for his own health. A lover does not usurp the responsibility of a beloved in life, nor should one do so in death. I pray, my love, that you put aside any responsibility that was mine and accept this comfort.

I am sure you know the truth of your regrets, yet this reflection may sound as though I need to convince you. I have emphasized the search for reality only because I have learned through Louise that freedom from the "if only" of grief can be a struggle. I ask that you also remember Louise. Be gentle with yourself, my love, and remember our love as you remember and test your regrets.

If I die suddenly, you may especially regret not having a chance to say a loving good-bye. Remember Uncle George.

He was dying for months but nobody admitted this truth to him because of our mixture of hope and denial. Of course, when he was too ill for either hope or denial, he was also too far gone to make his peace with anyone. In the end I suspect he died with unfinished business and without a final good-bye. If I do die suddenly, remember that a slower death would probably change nothing. I hope the words in my love-will help you make your good-bye whatever the circumstances of my death.

Peace Be with You

Remorse is the poison of life.

Charlotte Brontë

You may feel that some of your regrets are different. You may blame yourself, and all your reality testing does is pronounce sentence: guilty as charged. For any such regrets I must remind you that we both made many mistakes, and forgave each other many times as all lovers must. Death is bound to catch us with a need to forgive and be forgiven.

If you blame yourself, remember what Jesus said to His friends who were grieving and confused or who, like Peter, were suffering from guilt and self-reproach. He said, "Peace be with you," several times so they could absorb His message. Having passed death to stand looking back at a grieving humanity, would not the most inconsiderate person, with the smallest seed of love within, cry out in forgiveness and peace? When all things have passed away including our bad temper, thoughtlessness, and selfishness, surely if there were one word left to cry out from our human love that word would be peace.

Believe that only love survives and the words of love that echo from beyond the grave are "peace be with you." Peace, my love. You are unconditionally forgiven for any real or imagined wrongs, and I pray that you forgive yourself.

My Will Is Gone

Freedom is not something that anybody can be
given. Freedom is something people take, and
people are as free as they want to be.

James Baldwin

Recently we discussed redoing the house and I realized once again just how often I want things done my way. We agree on many issues but my will dominates on others. Needless to say, my will isn't always that of a lover. Sometimes I hold you back by not encouraging you and not desiring enough for you. I am sorry for the part of my will that is sometimes determined to have its way at your expense. Above all else, remember when you read these words that my selfish determination will be gone. However our wills may have clashed, mine will then be gone or one with God's. Whatever your way, it will be my desire for you. Don't seek to please me for I will always be pleased as you follow your way.

Yet my will may take on a new importance when I die. – At my funeral: "It's what he would have wanted"; Comforters: "He would have approved"; The lawyer: Reading his will. The images spring up naturally. They may offer you some comfort but it will be easy in your grief to make too much of them. My desire in this reflection is to show you the comfort, yet balance it with caution.

You may catch yourself saying "we" out of habit. Grief may seem at times to make me an addiction complete with withdrawal symptoms. Long after you have stopped saying "we," a part of you will likely still be thinking and doing "we." Our friends may fear you work too hard to do what you think I would want. But you may feel comforted by doing, if not with me, at least what we used to do. Doing some of the jobs I now do may be like putting on my old sweater and being surrounded, enfolded and comforted. If you do jobs for comfort, no lover would deny you even the little you might get from doing familiar tasks at the expense of an overtired body. But it's your decision. Do everything in your own way and in your own time. Don't do them for me because my will is gone.

Your self-preservation requires that you have a purpose to sustain you through the depths of your grief. Victor Frankl asserts that purpose is one of our greatest needs – that one can survive almost any hardship and suffering provided one can find meaning. He describes a widower who could not bear his grief until he realized that his wife would have had similar grief had he predeceased her. His suffering prevented her from similar suffering. Thus, it had a purpose and that made it bearable. Purpose is central to both mental and spiritual health. Perhaps reasons like "I must go on for the children. He would have wanted me to" will sustain you through the first painful weeks of grief when there is so little else.

Your path is narrow and you must find your way safely through the grey fog of your grief without becoming lost. Some of the comforting shapes in the fog are mirages of my will. They will be mirages because they have their origins now in you and not me. If you clasp onto them white-knuckled, they may only keep you in the fog instead of seeing you through. Take comfort from the shapes, but don't see them as real and give them life. The danger in refusing to let my will die is that my will will grow and harden. This is not love, but a form of mummification – a living in the past. The failing is in not struggling to create and love in a world that is continually creating and in which love is both our greatest gift and greatest need.

Social scientists advise not to make major decisions during a time of emotional crisis. Grief is a particularly vulnerable time because our will is not fully known. Take time to find your own will as you let go of our collective will. Our collective will had a particular flavour, part of what happened as we became one. Now, in your own time as you grieve, you must surrender it as you become more aware of your own will.

"He would turn over in his grave if he knew." What an awful expression! Well, I suppose it does have humour. But please don't make my will the temper tantrum of a spoiled child – strong-willed, determined to have his way. When my will is one with God's, it will desire you to be fully alive and all that you can be. It will surely rejoice and celebrate your recovery and independence.

It's odd that, on the one hand, friends may think I would disapprove when you do things differently than was our way, yet, on the other, fear you are hanging onto the past and advise you to get on with your own life. Confusion about the departed's will obviously runs deep.

The putting-on of the familiar, the habit of "we," and the need for a purpose all provide normal comfort that is universally used by the grieving. Accept the comfort. I have confidence in you that you will let my will go in your own time. I pray that this reflection helps you to understand and not to resist when my will slowly slips away.

I love the conviction and the determination of your will, for they are akin to the virtue of fortitude – a strength that I count on when I waver. But even more, I love the desire of your will, for it nurtures me. I am confident that your will will see you through your grief and continue to create you.

When You Dread the Nights

Turn Thou the key upon our thoughts,
dear Lord,
And let us sleep;
Give us our portion of forgetfulness,
Silent and deep.

Virna Sheard

You jokingly made me promise to get rid of our bed if you should predecease me. I laughed and said it's tit for tat. Yet how easy it is to take for granted the slumber and comfort from our bed, and how stark and sobering is the vision of the lovers' bed, half empty. How fortunate that we can take this pleasure for granted.

Perhaps before I die our snoring and fidgeting will drive us to twin beds or even to separate rooms. It doesn't matter. I write about sleep because there will be a new absence to face in your bed even if by chance my physical absence occurs many years before my death. But I expect we will keep our bed, for it is important to both of us.

A bed is, first of all, simply a bed – the word we knew as children and the place where we met our first biological need for sleep. The phrases "to be bedded" and "to sleep together" came later to represent the fulfilment of a second need. Yet, they are not just euphemisms for sex because language is much more complex, and we are not so pragmatic that we remain unaffected by our language. You will be affected too, my love. You desire the security of a simple house and the restful sleep of a child, but there is no returning to the innocence of child-hood. The sensual environment lives on, and unconsciously you will meet it nightly in the sleeplessness of your bed.

Picture a primitive tribe huddled in their cave by the fire at night. Pervasive smells and sounds of others fill the air with comfort. Contrast these caves with modern ones that separate the tribe by emphasizing privacy; not just privacy for the nuclear family, but for each member of the group. Even as babies we had our own private caves away from the master cave.

Then we married, shared a cave as husband and wife, and experienced again the primitive comfort of another in the darkness of the night. How quickly we adapted to each other's movements, to the turning, hugging, crowding, and hogging of blankets. Our comfort was not because we were afraid of the dark or even aware of the social legacy imprinted in our genes by our ancestors. Nor are you afraid, my love, but once again you are a social animal alone in your cave at night. Your tribal ancestry explains why it was easier to learn to sleep well with me, snorer and grunter that I may be, than to learn to sleep alone again in the absence of all the pleasures and irritations. Only one thing is more disruptive to sleep than stimuli from another and that is their sudden absence.

You wanted a dog, but I was never very keen to say the least. I didn't want to share your affections with a real beast with dog breath. If there were backs to be rubbed, I wanted to be the lucky animal. "I will grow more hair on my back," I joked. Now things will have changed and a dog might help. Our cat sleeping on your bed is more likely now to improve your night's sleep than to disturb it. In fact, even the television or the radio may be more conducive to sleep than silence. A pillow at your back or a special blanket can provide physical contact and comfort. I can only encourage you to experiment.

In grief, there is a withdrawal from the many chemicals from the skin of the other; a withdrawal from lovers' gifts exchanged by kisses and caresses. Lovers could not describe the chemicals and if pressed would name a perfume or cologne that was uniquely their mate's. But the unique perfumes are not from bottles on the dresser but manufactured daily and secreted through a thousand pores. Pervasive. Obtained in every stroke and nuzzle. They linger in the house, especially in the bed and clothes. But they fade with time until the body no longer obtains its chemical cues and must adapt to their absence.

Yes, loneliness is aggravated by chemistry. But your body will strike a new balance in the absence of my scent. That is life: dynamic, changing, adjusting, and adapting. Neither worse nor better in the absence of my chemistry, but different: in another state that is better suited for the new environment of my absence.

My desire is for you to understand that your body as well as your mind is adjusting to my absence from your bed. When pain must be borne, comfort can be taken from simply understanding it.

Going to sleep presents a catch-22. You must cross the bridge from your mind's busy day and drift into sleep without giving your mind free rein to chase a thousand memories. You have to be set aside the activities of your day, but then your resistance drops and you are flooded with memories and a pervasive absence. You may fall asleep in your chair, yet be wide awake moments after going to bed. When sleep does come, it may be cat naps that fail to fully restore you. Most grievers say that it wouldn't be so bad if it wasn't for the nights. Activity keeps memories at bay but not at night. They become hounds – uncontrolled – baying and chasing the scent of a thousand trails.

Some people drive themselves to exhaustion and then collapse in bed, turn off, shut out, flake out, sink into oblivion. Sometimes this works but often, though, it just increases their thirst for physical and mental comfort. Although the gauntlet of memories is shorter, it must still be run! Sleeplessness may only be compounded with a bone-weary fatigue. Perhaps there is some comfort in knowing that your sleeplessness is natural, and in knowing that sleep will become easier as you slowly deal with the memories.

You may fear another sleepless night with your memories and only yourself for company. This may become a self-fulfilling fear that steals sleep. What to do? I pray that you neither drug yourself into submission nor suffer to exhaustion. Accept that in your sleepless nights you are doing the grief work that will lead to your recovery. The sleeplessness is not all bad. I pray that you come to see the purpose and that it makes your sleeplessness more bearable.

Bed time is our normal time for quietly taking stock. A routine is easier to adjust than to discard and so I pray that you will develop your own routine of reading, relaxing, and reflecting on your day. Perhaps you will be able to reflect, too, on a few memories and let them pass. Better still, if you can write a few notes about our life and the present pain for that would be grief work supreme, and a prayer most holy.

View Our Relationship as a Gift

The Gods themselves cannot recall their gifts.
Alfred, Lord Tennyson

Today is our anniversary so it seems appropriate to reflect on gifts. We were "given in marriage" as our greatest gift to each other. When the string of pearls I gave you on our wedding day was stolen, this did not destroy my original act of giving, nor did it destroy me. You still remember the gift and I am still the giver. Things don't last forever and neither do our lives. Living our relationship is like reading a novel. The ending cannot change the part that has been read. That part is history set in print upon the pages. Take comfort in remembering the part of our gift that cannot be destroyed by death.

When I am gone the material gifts that remain may seem like cold artifacts without a ray to warm them for, however cherished, they will likely not be so important as the absence of the intangible gifts of my attention, conversation, and presence – our daily giving. It may seem a painful vacuum. A vacuum draws substance in to fill the space or else shrinks it till it is only sufficient to hold that which remains. Both things will likely happen in your grief. Family and friends will come to fill your space and time, but the shrunken emptiness may sometimes seem more than you can bear.

This is a painful image, but please don't turn away because I think you may gain comfort from this image. The comfort lies in the perspective of time. All our connections are imperfect and are gained slowly through our giving. Ours took courtship and years of marriage. But we have connected in many ways, so by comparison no friends may be close enough to fill your emptiness. To be fulfilled, more gifts of life must be exchanged with them. In time friends will connect to fill the vacuum. Their love will redefine and fill your space. Take comfort in new connections as they grow, for therein lies your comfort. I join the gentle urging of our Creator. Give. Love. Connect.

View All My Things as Gifts

When the survivor is suddenly the recipient of
death benefits the new financial gain can cause
tremendous guilt.

Carol S. Staudacher

I give you everything I have when I am gone. When you clean the closets, you will make the easy decisions. Later you will need to truly sort to find your balance of remembrances and space. As you transform our space into your space, see all my things that surround you as gifts, for this will remind you that they were freely given with love and that everything is yours with complete freedom to do with as you like. All that calls forth thoughts like "He would have wanted me to keep this," signifies remnant strings. Perfect unconditional love has no strings and neither do perfect gifts. They cannot own you. I pray that you accept this freedom and that it gives you comfort.

If I leave imperfect gifts, as I probably will, this negates neither the reality of perfect gifts nor my parting wish to make them so. But, this does not mean they must be forever treasured, polished, and displayed like silver trinkets on the mantel. I mean perfect so you are free to enjoy them as you like or to give them away. But you may fear that in giving things away you will also give away your past. Also, discarding some things may seem a sacrilege to love. To all of these concerns, I urge you to remember that all the things I leave you are gifts that are freely given. Please don't make them bonds to provoke "should's" and guilt.

Many people feel guilty when they gain financially from a partner's death. They feel in some irrational way that they have cheated their spouses out of the fruits of their labour. Remember, my love, it is death that will cheat me out of the future we planned, not you. We worked hard together to raise our family and plan for the future. Our financial planning was a gift we gave each other. My legal will says it is yours, and my love-will says it is a gift with no strings attached. Please, no guilt.

I may have dwelled too long on freedom, but it is only because many people have lost the meaning of gifts. They give gifts with strings attached for retrieving them later or give gifts that control or manipulate in subtle ways. They may also expect us to keep gifts to show the giver that they are valued. Yet, a lover wants to give unconditionally, and understands that the gift that is given again to another is no less a gift or is it necessarily less cherished.

Accept everything as true gifts given solely for your pleasure. Treasure or share the material gifts as you like, for the love with which I gave them will always be yours.

Celebrate Your Life

Our task is to say a holy yes to the real things
of our life as they exist . . .

Natalie Goldberg

Today I recall the excitement of our wedding day. It was a new beginning full of promise and a new adventure like starting out on a lifetime trip together. Thank you for the adventure and thank you for celebrating the good and the bad along the way with me.

Our wedding day didn't make our marriage, so the day didn't have to be just right or be lost forever. Our marriage was made as we lived it and celebrated it daily. Our wedding pictures are no more our marriage than our vacation was the picture of us smiling and waving as we started out. These snapshots just marked a starting point. When we renewed our wedding vows, it was not a repeat celebration. We remembered our wedding, but we celebrated our marriage journey. We said a holy yes to the marriage we built. What we celebrated as a promise on our wedding day, we could celebrate as our bond.

We remember our marriage union through the weddings of our family and friends. The simple beauty of their vows always touched us. Sometimes we shed a tear or two. Our tears came from an inner place that was touched by the promise and by the love that was so visible. In fact, as wedding guests we were freed from all the distractions of our wedding day and could see the full meaning of marriage. We celebrated ours anew as we celebrated theirs.

Our celebrations have changed throughout our marriage. Sometimes our daily celebrations are with family and friends and sometimes alone with candlelight and wine. Often they are a spontaneous holy yes like lovemaking in the middle of the night, but sometimes in our struggles they are merely our endurance. All our celebrations are important for as we celebrate our marriage grows. Even when the fire is low we still celebrate our homey union. We always remember our wedding anniversaries and still celebrate them with gifts and often with tender loving.

Celebration is a model for all of life – not just living it, but celebrating it, and not just the good times but the changing moments of time. It's the dance of life, yet death is a part of life and so is grief. Please don't let my death end with a numbing funeral or in bitter grief. Like our first yes on our wedding day, the funeral will be just a start on another journey. Each celebration will be different and change your grief as it carries you further on your journey.

Some celebrations may be planned with your church community or other groups, but more likely they will just be spontaneous at gatherings of family and friends. You can share remembrances, pain, and laughter. Such are life and health, not just for you, but for the whole family, and especially the young. It is important that they see grief changing and resolving. This will help them resolve their own grief and equip them to deal with future pain.

My desire in giving you the image of celebrating life in the midst of your grief is to comfort you. I pray that celebrating may keep you from getting stuck in your grief.

These themes of celebrating and freedom come together beautifully in Anthony DeMello's simple prayer for freedom. It is a prayer of thanksgiving and separation that can be worded to help with any loss. Your prayer could be: How lucky I was that you came into my life. How grateful I am to you for all the years that we shared in our marriage. I will love you always but I must go. I have a life to live and a destiny to fulfill. Good-bye.

If You Write to Me

*Then at night I would write to Davy about
them: I was still writing to her, still with a sense
of writing to a real person. I even hoped — hoped
intensely — that she would, somehow, know
what I said.*

Sheldon Vanauken

You may recall that I used to keep notebooks in which I wrote
about the ups and downs of my life. Yesterday I came across a
beautiful book with gold-embossed covers that friends gave
me when they learned I kept a journal. It only had a few reflections and the rest was blank. Now I remember why. The book
was too good for my scribbling. I organized a few reflections
on scraps of paper and copied them into my book, but this
became tedious and I soon gave up my reflective writing.

Now if someone were to give me such a book, I would
begin with a humorous piece about my problem with intestinal
gas. I would write in sentence fragments, repeat myself, and
leave my spelling mistakes. I would be FREE — no longer intim-

idated by clean white pages in a book too nice to spoil with spontaneous celebration. I would frolic with feelings and words from the midst of my life. The words would be mostly ordinary, but sometimes an inspired prayer. This is how I wrote in my old books and I remember how it helped me reflect on my day. Writing helped me sort out my feelings and was good medicine for my spirit. Perhaps reflective writing or keeping a journal will help you in your grief. If you write, my love, just be yourself.

It has been said that an unexamined life is not worth living and that to write is to live life twice. The first time in real life we are too busy to live the moment fully or to think about it, but the moment isn't lost. We can experience it again by actually getting inside the memory with all its joy or pain and celebrating with chuckles or tears. We can stretch one moment of reality and experience it until we figure out what it means and let it challenge us and lead us onward.

Writing may help you capture an elusive part of yourself and fence it in with words so you can study it – perhaps even domesticate it. This may lead you deeper into the wild woods of your feelings and thoughts. Perhaps you will be able to see a situation clearly on a few sheets of paper. You can crumple the sheets and toss them on the fire, or keep them as a record of growth, like chalk marks on the wall. You have power to destroy and start again. But don't keep trying to get it right.

Just write till you are satisfied, and if it becomes a burden for you, then let it go. If you write, be gentle with yourself. My desire of love is only that you celebrate to find your truth.

If you have a problem writing to a piece of paper then try writing to me. Don't attempt to capture your whole life in a single poem unless that is your style. Just reflect about any event, memory, or feeling and go wherever your writing takes you. Your writing will eventually come less from your pain. You will gain a better perspective of situations and keep true to yourself.

Believe, my love, that reflective writing is a form of prayer and is surely answered with healing and peace.

When You Miss Me as a Friend

When your spouse has also been your best friend, you experience a loss which has many components.

Carol S. Staudacher

We went for a walk this Sunday afternoon as we especially like to do in the fall when the leaves are turning colour. The trail was one of our favourites and the colours were at their peak. We kicked the fallen leaves along the trail to a tea house in the next village where we had a coffee and a chat before our return. We had a splendid day.

Our day gave me cause to reflect on our friendship. We are good friends so I will write to you specifically as your friend, for I imagine that when I am gone your pain at the loss of me as your friend will be nearly as great as the loss of me as your lover. These pains will be one for you; in fact, I doubt that anyone could separate such loss.

You will remember that Sundays were hard days for my mother in her grief. For years my parents laboured in their shop and had little time for each other. Sunday was their day of rest when they kept their friendship. Our special times of friendship will likely also become your hardest times – our Sunday afternoons, breakfasts out, and vacations in the mountains. Our friendship is about the things we enjoyed doing together at our leisure. Our times of companionship will be especially empty for you.

Our friendship has its past – the memories – which you will still have. But even these may seem empty, for memories made with a friend are shared treasures until the friend is gone. Then the memories are like closets full of souvenirs that only the collectors can truly appreciate. The death of a friend is the death of a co-owner of memories – of intangible souvenirs. You mourn the loss of someone by your side – your present and your future. But you also mourn a loss in your past, for memories are made to be shared and I am the only one who knows of the memories made on our Sunday walks together.

Friends may remind you that we had many good years together, as if treasures from our friendship were secure in a bank. They may speak as if grief were merely a present moment and an empty future. Yet you know that grief for a friend is all encompassing. Its depth can be inconsolable precisely because it embraces not only the present and future but also your past. In foreseeing this loss for you, I can only acknowledge it and offer support and encouragement. I trust you will find these abundantly in my love-will.

My desire is not to glorify our friendship for it will fade when I am gone. Besides, I don't know the future, so I can only pray that we always remain good friends. My desire is to offer some support for when I am gone. May it help you grieve our friendship.

Friendship didn't fuse us to make us identical. I simply enjoy your uniqueness, and doing things with you along the margins where our interests touch. Although a poor companion for some activities, you have other friends with whom you do things you don't do with me. These other friendships will not be lost when I die and will comfort you in your grief. True friendships welcome other friends. They are always inclusive and they snowball by inviting others. Many friends remain when a spouse dies. In fact, two in friendship are not two, or even three, but many! I pray that these friendships give you comfort. My friendship-prayer for you is that I become ever less while your other friends become ever more. Any loving friend before his passing would pray this prayer of self-death.

When I die, the future of our friendship will also die, but it will be remembered. Your perception of the past and future will change with each passing day as you travel down your road. A friend is one who goes with you down that road and is a bridge to your future. As your friend, I pray that you feel me with you at least a short way down your new road. I also pray that through my love-will I will be part of your bridge to your future.

Finding New Meaning in Life

I don't know what kind of future life I believe in,
but I believe that all that we go through here
must have some value.

Eleanor Roosevelt

I am a little discouraged as I write this reflection. A business proposal I have been working on for weeks was returned for more work. The project seems to be bogged down and I am not sure where it is going. I find it hard to keep an interest in moving it forward.

I suspect you will often be discouraged and feel that life is without meaning. Discouragement is a part of grief. In fact, it can have the emptiness, slowed pace and lack of energy of depression. Scripture advises us to trust, to hope, and to endure whatever comes, but sometimes we get tired and discouraged and our spirits seem unwilling. Perhaps you lack the energy and spirit now to rally. If so, I urge you to be patient with yourself and shorten your stride to one day at a time, for love is patient and kind.

I pray that your life moves from discouragement to meaning. I am reluctant to acknowledge discouragement because I do not want to add to any you may feel. Yet I cannot ignore it, for the desire of love is to lend support. I will keep the watch with you. It heartens me that the vigil with you in this love-will is more important than my words.

If you had died before me, I would likely have endured by burying myself in work to keep meaning in my life. But your meaning comes more through your relationships than mine does, so I imagine you will turn to others. Perhaps this difference explains why young husbands survive grief better than young wives. However, in older relationships, the wives fare much better. Most men fail to take the time to cultivate relationships that would feed their spirits. Meaning is hard for them to find when their career is over and death takes away their nurturing wives. In fact, some people without good relationships are unable to survive the grief of retirement. There is nothing or no one to fill their void of emptiness.

Perhaps turning to relationships will be harder for you in the short term than burying yourself in work. But take comfort, my love, for relationships will ultimately help restore you. My desire is not a call for you to bury yourself in your work or to overcommit yourself with friends. Yet I urge you

on to find new meaning in both your work and your relationships.

We think that encouragement is the opposite of discouragement, but perhaps the opposite is a willing spirit. We can
easily forget an encouragement but a willing spirit is encouragement that has come home and taken root. It is a willing
spirit that helps provide us meaning and helps us live in faith.

Our language blinds us to our need for action. We use
words like love, death, grief, and dozens of others as simple
nouns when they are bursting with action. Life itself is nothing
except the action of living. The action in the verbs to live, to
love, to die, to grieve, to comfort, and to heal gives us the
meaningful nouns: life, love, death, grief, comfort, and health.
Truly the meaning is in the action. And yet, many lonely people look for something when to fill their emptiness they must
first do something.

The call to action is the same for you in your grief as for all
people – an exhortation. Grief is not meant to be a painful
state of inaction but a call to action. This call is the same
whether it is the advice of the helping profession, the teaching
of Scripture, or the counsel of a lover. I urge you to live in the
full meaning of the word in relationships with all our family
and friends. From this action you will get what you need and
restore your willing spirit that gives your life meaning.

I pray that you feel the love from these words for love

gives meaning to all things. In closing, I leave you a promise of support and also an encouragement. For support, know that I am with you always in the spirit of love, and all encouragement is but the urging of love. This is my love-will; all of it is my exhortation to you, my love. I pray that it provides you comfort through support and encouragement as you struggle to find new meaning in your life.

Feeling Whole Again

*Only in a free space can re-creation take place
and new life be found.*

Henri Nouwen

Who am I to write of wholeness? I often fail at the very task of integration that will lie before you in your grief. My health demands that I integrate exercise and new, healthier eating habits into my life, but I simply diet to lose a few pounds then return to my old eating habits. It isn't that I object to exercise either. It's just that I want to do it once, at some convenient time, and be done with it. So in writing to you, I must confront my own failings in embracing wholeness.

By human nature we are all addicted to quick solutions as we struggle to reach the succession of dangling carrots in our lives. But life invites us to live solutions and to enjoy the process. Spiritually, some Christians speak of being born again.

Yet we miss the truism that rebirths occur in all successful life changes. Our marriage itself was a rebirth. It wasn't something tacked onto our separate lives from time to time, but something born and lived. Everything that is not born and integrated into the wholeness of our lives will be abandoned like my diet.

Your life may be too busy, yet too empty. You are probably patching your life and hanging on, whereas my desire of love is that you listen to the counsel of your heart and embrace the wholeness of new life. I encouraged you earlier not to make significant changes until you are sure of your own will. Later your very restlessness will be an invitation to review your life. There may be a creative tension between your restless human nature to complete and an urging from within to integrate and live. Trust that when your emotional storms of grief begin to pass, you will be reborn to wholeness in a new life.

Henri Neuwen expresses our need for free space. But loneliness is such an omnipotent, painful, and frightening prospect that we may fail to appreciate the positive value of solitude. As May Sarton asserts in *I Knew a Phoenix*, "Solitude is one thing and loneliness another." The free space of spiritual solitude is bright and restful, whereas loneliness is dark and empty. A task of life is to find our restful solitude without the fear of loneliness. But the task is difficult in grief because the essence of grief is spiritual turmoil in a place of empty darkness. Have faith that in time you will find your solitude.

I am writing about wholeness for this word has useful imagery. There is no wholeness in loneliness, for the very ache is for something that is lacking. But neither is there wholeness in the busy life that I imagine has sustained you through your grief. Your busy life may drain you and trap you in an endless string of days spent simply enduring life. I hope that sharing my understanding of our need for wholeness has helped.

Moving towards wholeness may require some changes to make your life easier and more satisfying. If so, only you can decide what is best for you. I cannot comfort you by providing solutions, but you will find them close at hand during your solitude in the counsel of your own heart. Slow down and accept its counsel. Let it heal your busy life so you may live your life more completely. Friends cannot take away your loneliness. You must do it yourself by transforming it into solitude. I pray that you find your inner place of solitude and rest. Listen to its counsel for its words are healing. Such an inner journey is not selfish, but is the source of your own strength, direction, and creating. To paraphrase Nouwen, even the longing of our hearts is from God and to touch this longing is to be touched by the healing hand of God. I pray that you touch it and are touched.

I have not called you a widow very often because its imagery does not hold the space you need. The word is too passive, too static, and definitely too final for your rebirth. It is a label for someone who is incomplete – a married woman forever without her man, some fraction left behind by death. You are a person and that is a better word because it leaves you whole. In marriage we each became part of a mysterious whole of which you are the surviving person. Through grief you are gradually letting go your departed half and making your life whole. Perhaps it's like two perfect, rubber spheres pressed together till they are flattened where they meet. When one sphere is removed the other resumes it shape for it always was a sphere. There is healing in remembering that you are a complete and loving person and you always were.

Your previous companions of grief and widowhood will leave you, but your personhood gives you full freedom and a whole, loving future wherever it may take you. In travelling with personhood you will come to know your whole self again. You never know a friend until she is accepted, travelled with, and learned from. This is your rebirth to wholeness – the difference between accepting your present condition and living it, between short and long term, between existence and life fully lived, and immediate solutions and a prayerful quest.

A lover's desiring is not for wholeness in his limited vision but wholeness that is the reborn other. I urge you on in your search for wholeness. I pray that my love-will helps clear a restful space for you. I invite you always to enter this loving space in solitude, to disarm yourself, and to find your counsel.

You May Experience My Presence

Nearly all of 22 young and middle-aged
widows reported experiencing the presence of
their dead husbands in some way . . . Studies
of widows in England . . . and in Japan . . .
yielded similar results and examples.

Richard A. Kalish

I often point out older couples and comment on how much they look alike. Some look like Bobbsey twins in matching outfits, but others actually bear a physical resemblance to each other. They're slap happies, sour pusses, or what have you. And what a hoot when their dog has the same expression. "Do you suppose we're beginning to look alike?" I joked today and smiled to prime our familiar routine. You didn't disappoint.

"Oh no, how boring!" you exclaimed in mock horror, and we had a private chuckle.

Perhaps responding to shared experiences does produce similar expressions. In any case, we are growing together in our love and in many ways we have become one. We laugh at the same jokes and suffer from the same family pain. One of us does not hurt without the other hurting, nor will one of us die without a death in the other. But we are spared the boredom of sameness because we really are quite different. The desire of love is not to grow a twin but to develop and enjoy the full potential of each other. Thank you for our coupleness.

Our coupleness or oneness may have an unusual consequence. In your grief, you may see me as if in a dream, but when you are awake. Our ancestors accepted such visions but they seem out of place and are seldom mentioned in our age of science. How sad, for such visions are normal and they are experienced by lovers around the world. Comfort can be taken from them, yet they can cause confusion. No lover could remain silent, nor can I. Let's seek the comfort.

Did you know that an amputee may continue to feel a missing limb? We too are one flesh. Will you sense my presence in your grief like some amputees do their limbs? Will an amputee effect explain my presence after death or will it be me making my good-bye? That's a mystery, but does it really matter to your comfort. If either explanation comforts you, use it; if not, then let it pass. The important thing is that the images are normal; you will not be going crazy.

Perhaps you would feel more comfort if assured that my presence would be real. Yet my words fall short. Although any images of me will be normal and real, I will be dead and even the images are temporary and will pass. It will be impossible for us to be together again in this life. Love asks you to let the images of me simply be, to let them flow over you and give you comfort. But love also asks you to let go because they are a farewell and not a welcome.

I just called the images real, but what is real? Is love itself unreal because it can neither be seen nor touched, nor measured with scientific instruments? Are your images of me any more real if they are an amputation effect?

There are no scientific tools to extract proofs about such images because they are shrouded in mystery. Our many churches with their tools of prayer and faith are better equipped but they are also quiet about such images even though they are almost universally experienced in grief. Such silence must not to be taken as a denial of the reality of your experiences. Our churches are just reluctant to talk about images and visions in today's world. Yet the history of most faiths includes visions. Still, you may hesitate to tell friends of your experience, and rightly so, because they may not understand. Accept the images as a gift for you if that is comforting. When in my own grief I was overwhelmed with a vision bringing comfort and peace, I recalled the Beatitude: "Blessed are they that mourn for they shall be comforted."

May my words, as inadequate as they are, give you comfort. I pray that you accept comfort from any images of me and that you integrate them into your faith through prayer and reflection. Accept mystery in life. Live with mystery. Believe there is infinitely more to the universe, and even to humankind, than we can comprehend. Accept life, and even death, with awe. Accept, too, from our faith that if and when you see me, my love, it will be to bring peace and to comfort you in your grief.

When You Help Another

By remembering one's grief and accepting it,
one grows in warmth, in understanding
and in wisdom.

Lynn Caine

I remember when we helped a widowed friend through her grief. My recent memory of Virginia prompts me to write this reflection for my love-will.

Many men abdicate responsibility for nurturing others to women. While I hesitated and wondered what to say to grieving friends, you acted naturally out of your caring. Through you I learned that our specific reaction to the pain of others is not as important as doing something timely out of love. Thank you for all I learned from you.

In an earlier reflection on wholeness, you may have become aware of your progress and healing. Perhaps you feel ready to reach out again to a grieving friend who is in need. It will not be the same as when we lent an ear to Virginia, for this time your grieving friend will trigger the full feelings of your own loss. You will be keenly aware of both those who supported you in your grief and of your desire to help another. We can never fully empathize with a fellow sufferer until we have experienced their pain. You will now understand grief and will have lost any neutrality in the presence of another's. Our compassion makes us more human, yet it is born of our pain and of that of others.

Perhaps helping someone will give some meaning to your own pain, but I will not suggest a specific purpose. I think that no lover should ever speak of purpose in such matters except for himself. The purpose for all others is their sacred mystery. We should approach this mystery in others with gentleness and reverence. Yet I feel that our whole lives have a purpose, even our grief. I pray that you find your purpose and accept its comfort. The alternative makes grief an especially empty place.

Many widowed people come to help others in their grief and this marks a milestone in their recovery. I imagine that you will do the same, so I want to share some thoughts that might be comforting.

I imagine that you will feel good about giving something of yourself to help another. It's natural, yet perhaps you feel you should receive no pleasure in helping. Truly, grief makes a jealous god. It can complicate every good feeling and, if allowed, pervert it. Mere pleasure through involvement in another's suffering would be a sin, but love is not. We are blessed when our response to the pain of others is love, for love redeems us by restoring our self-worth. It is normal if you are happy, yes even joyful, in your re-creation. People often get involved in social action to meet some of their own needs. However, you may have a nagging feeling that it's selfish because there is something in it for you.

Love calls me to counter this implication for if it were true, we would do nothing. Love would be a sterile act, not the core of the mystery that creates us and gives us eternal life. To be needed is a basic human need. This is why a good support group is so effective. We go to it empty and without pretense in our need, and we go not knowing whether the group needs us. Yet, in our need we are genuine and thus available for each other. This is close to the paradox of life that there is strength in our weakness and that in giving we receive. All is a gift. Need itself is a gift.

There is something for us in reaching out. That is always the way. We reach out with our gift only to discover later that we are being gifted. This is love, the echo. All our loving gives us a gift in one way or another, as long as receiving is not our main purpose. In fact, Mystery calls us to reflect upon each day to hear the echo and learn what life is asking of us. All our service can then become a gift from which to learn our truth. My prayer is that you let go naturally of grief so that you may reach out in love and take pleasure in your gifts.

Besides the pleasure of giving, you will gain perspective. A newly widowed person taps you on your shoulder in your grief. You turn only to realize that you are not caught in a maze as it seemed in your grief, but have been travelling down a long, winding road. All our paths seem different when we look back. This truth is in the woodsman's rule that if you want to find your way out of the woods, then glance over your shoulder as you walk in.

You may also see yourself like an old, yellowed snapshot from the family album. It makes you realize how much you have changed. Although you recognize the picture, it is no longer you. Your grief has changed. There is comfort from this discovery as you look back, for through the pain of others we find the truth of our own. Because the pain is secondhand, we are not so likely to turn away before we have seen it clearly. Self-discovery is more likely, too, because they haven't travelled as far down the road. If you were both just starting your journey of grief you might lose your perspective and not be as helpful to each other. But there is little fear of this, for in the first pain of grief we turn inward, not outward to another.

Reach out, my love, when you feel ready. Lend an attentive ear, for now you know its importance in grief. Just as there is grief in love, there is also love in grief. I pray that you accept the gifts of being needed and of healing.

You Are Beautiful

Love is a great beautifier.

Louise May Alcott

Today I saw an elderly woman of particular charm and grace who inspired me to write about beauty. She had grown old gracefully, and I imagined that she had loved so consistently well that love now dwelled within. Hers was not the beauty of youth but that of gracious warmth. Little crow's feet only enhanced the warm sparkle of her eyes and nothing could hide her inner glow. Her sexuality was not flaunted, yet was not forgotten. She was confident and mature. In her I saw the seed of youthful beauty in its ripened fruit. Her beauty was like that of a golden field of wheat – matured through the seasons and ready to yield an abundant gift for others.

Love ages well. I have no doubt that you will age like the

older woman that I admired. Do not fear the passing years for I am sure you will mature like fine wine. I love you as you are and how you grow. Don't fear, for love worn well gives lasting beauty.

My prayer for you is that you age with love's beauty; that love will soften any lines I may etch upon you, into life's beauty marks. May young men look upon you and know that love's beauty stands the test of time.

We have much to build in our allotted time, and lovers know the importance of their creation. They know that, most importantly, they must build themselves as you have always done. No one sees the beauty of another's creation like a fellow builder. For lovers, it is a pleasure to see another lover as a model – to see in some older other a magnificent, selfless self-creation.

Longing of Our Hearts

Be not afraid of life. Believe that life is worth
        living,
and your belief will help create the fact.
            William James, *The Will to Believe*

As I write today, I remember our courting days when we shared
our understanding of life as lovers do. The fire of our love
made that a special time. I hope this love is never lost, but
warms us through all our days. Nor should it be lost in your
grief for the dreams of lovers are important. They are a legacy.
My love-will would be incomplete without sharing about the
fire of love that continues to create us.

This reflection is a gift of myself shared in love. It is not
shared to become your dream for every lover has his own. My
desire is only to help you find the fire of love in your grief
because life can be cold without it.

I struggle to reconcile religion, medicine, and science, and

I imagine in your grief that you will search for meaning in all of life. The root is our Creator. Religion embodies our relationship with Him, whereas medicine and science are one step removed. Medicine deals with the health and healing of His creatures, and science with unravelling the mysteries of His creation. This simplistic view helps me keep God central, and helps me see my first vocation as being a lover. But if the root is God, as we accept by faith, I feel there should be a comforting and unifying trace of God within us and in each discipline. Yet how easy it is in medicine and science to lose sight of God without our first vocation as a lover.

I found that the unifying trace, which gives me wholeness, is like the longing of my heart. I share it now for this longing is important for all lovers and it even bridges death. People of prayer, medicine, and science have all glimpsed something omnipresent, omnipotent, and beyond the dimension of time. They have glimpsed God through longing in words like attitude, consciousness, will, desire, and prayer.

Within me, there is the longing that is prayer. My faith teaches that this longing comes from the spirit. I was slow to name this longing and to let it be a prayer. Your spirit, too, has its prayer; our roots are intertwined. They know no death. I believe this attitude is what Saint Paul meant when he urged us to pray continuously.

Most doctors acknowledge that they only help the body

mend itself. They accept that our attitude, will, and prayers influence our recovery. This attitude, which is so important in medicine, creates and heals, as does our spiritual longing.

Scientists discovered that desiring an outcome can influence an experiment and even a computer. The effects of desiring and consciousness are like prayer. Remarkably, the desiring can be done from afar and at a different time. This is like the prayer of our faith that bridges the dimensions of time and space. It is exciting that science has also discovered something that bridges time and space, and that it is like our longing and our prayer.

Perhaps this reflection encourages us to pray simply, yet not to consider our prayers and their answers as cause and effect, but more at the level of the inseparable whole that scientists now consider. In reality we know little of God except what He has revealed to us through time and, through Jesus, what He is like in human form.

I have shared a small dream of my reality. It includes religion, medicine, and science; it breaks the dimensions of time and space. It is as simple as the longing of my heart, but as far beyond my imaginings as the inseparable whole and quantum physics. It's open-ended: leaves God an uncreated Mystery and us in a universe without walls. The root is our longing and our prayer – our connection with God and universe, the inseparable whole. My dream can hold all lovers' dreams and it creates from their very longing. Lovers feel the poetic truth of Tennyson, "More things are wrought by prayer than this world dreams of." As I write, I appreciate how much your loving me and desiring the best for me is a prayer that creates me.

Please don't confuse longing with pining. Longing embraces what is bigger than oneself. It celebrates and creates. It helps keep one outward bound. Pining turns one inward in decline to languish, wither, and waste.

Are the longings of lovers so very different from the prayers of the saints? I believe, my love, that we will always be connected in the Mystery of the inseparable whole through the longing of our hearts. I pray that you see the creative power of your attitude, desire, and loving, and that this fire of love continues to create you.

Your Need for Intimacy

> *. . . nobody dies from lack of sex. It's lack of*
> *love we die from. There's nobody here I can love,*
> *all the people I could love are dead or elsewhere.*
> **Margaret Atwood**, *The Handmaid's Tale*

In thinking about intimacy, I can't help but reflect on ours. As compared with sex, I have been slower in learning the full meaning of intimacy. Perhaps, like many men, I am too goal-oriented for intimacy is time together with no particular goal – more like loving than sex. I'm learning about taking the time to talk, to share dreams, hopes and fears, to pray together, and to hold each other. I only hope I am learning enough to meet your needs.

You will need to invest more in others to meet your needs when I am gone. My wish is to help you let go of me and to provide some comfort for that time whenever it may be.

I have always called you my love since our courting days.

It's my term of endearment and I continue to use it out of habit. Perhaps when we were young our love was too exclusive, but even then I hope no ownership was taken. But, be assured as you read my love-will that if I ever seemed possessive that too has passed away. I hope there never was a cage, but if there was, it's gone. Any possessiveness you may feel now is from your grief and not the reality of love. There are no barriers to new intimate relationships. I pray that you feel free to develop them as you need.

"What she needs is a good loving." Have you heard this expression? Doesn't everyone? Need a good loving, that is – at least in the meaning of giving and accepting intimacy. And yet, the good loving has been perverted to mean sex. The quotation from *The Handmaid's Tale* puts sex in its proper place. The handmaid's lament is not a pity party, "no one loves me," but rather the lover within her crying out for somebody to love. We lump the giving and taking in relationships together and call it all love. It's interesting that we name the giver of love the lover, but the receiver, the beloved, sounds archaic.

I think the distinction between the giver and receiver of love is important for we easily confuse the two needs. Some distinguish love as gift or as need, but giving love is also a human need, and any need to love is a precious gift. A sponge is for soaking up what we need and a fountain for giving to others. You will need to be a fountain and invest in others to pass the final stage of grief. It's also what life demands of lovers. The paradox of love is most beautifully expressed in the prayer of Saint Francis: "in giving we receive."

I suspect that, like the handmaid, your greater need now is to give love. But your need to give may not always be appreciated by your friends. In fact, if you do something thoughtful for them, they may say that you shouldn't have, not with what you are going through. But after "poor me" and "no one loves me," the real need becomes someone to love. That is the real emptiness. Perhaps it is comforting to recognize that our need to love is there for a reason and to thank God for it. This need will help keep you outward focused and open to new relationships.

Some people invest in a pet to help with fountain needs. It is important to them to have something in the house that misses them and that needs them. If a pet will help, get one, but I must add one caution. Remember Mrs. Morley – her dog became an excuse to stay at home and her social connections dried up. In the end her dog owned her. So please, my love, keep a pet in perspective and don't trade off long-term needs for short-term gains. People need people.

Now I will turn from the fountain to considering the sponge. I imagine your friends will invite you out; however, the invitations may stop too quickly. People so very much underestimate our need for love to fill the vacuum that can go on for months. Outwardly you look better to them, so they think you must be better. Perhaps they also fear that you will become dependent and they want you to make your own life.

Adults don't touch each other much in our society. And yet you need to be touched. You need to receive physical love. How slow professionals were to learn that babies needed to be touched. In experiments, orphaned babies were given the best of modern physical care and still they died. Many more survived when they were also touched and held. One does not outgrow such an early and basic need. Does your body ache to be touched and held? Like the babies' need, it is not sexual but a human need for physical contact.

"I just want to crawl in a hole and die." Not just die, but crawl in a hole first! Are we, after all, cryptophilic – like cockroaches and other little creatures that hide in tight spaces? Must we make sensory contact or else feel exposed and scurry into our private little holes to die?

There is no denying our needs for physical intimacy. But where are the hugs and the pats on the back that keep you from crawling into your hole? Such intimacies will be less acceptable with married friends in our social circle. Then again, how many single people are our friends? Not many. Married couples tend to socialize together and exclude the single or widowed. They are either unaware of their basic needs or else label them as sexual and a threat. Be aware that your physical needs are normal – that it is society that has connected them so inseparably with sex. It is difficult for contact between the sexes to be mere intimacy when one is single.

Let me return to you, for you cannot change society. There may be a counterpart in you that avoids intimacy. Some widows avoid intimacy because it feels to them a bit like being unfaithful. This avoidance complicates grief and suspends their comfort. Lest this be the case with you, my love, let me be direct. Don't avoid intimate friends. Acknowledge that you are a sensual person. Enjoy your friends. Give to them and receive from them.

Your needs in grief may not be met by our circle of friends. You may need to cultivate new friends or invest in new groups such as those for singles and widowed. May you feel free to reach out to others for physical contact, but not be driven into sexual intimacy before you are ready. I pray that I have helped you be aware of your physical need for intimacy and that you feel free to give and receive love.

Give all our friends a hug for me.

Consider Remarriage

> *. . . to have and to hold, for better or for worse,*
> *in sickness and in health . . . forsaking all*
> *others, till death do you part.*
>
> **Marriage vows**

We went to another wedding yesterday. The groom was my uncle, a widower of eighty-two, and the bride was a widow of seventy-eight who had lost her mate two years ago. Both families were so happy that they had found each other. I have already written about the need and the gift of intimacy and of its importance for mental and spiritual health. Their marriage prompts me to go further and reflect on remarriage.

Although these words are for a future time, I suspect that you will read my whole love-will shortly after my death. I hope my words don't seem inappropriate. Let me assure you that our marriage is important and our love helped create me. I pray that this is evident throughout my love-will so that I can now turn to the future without fear of hurting you. There is no correct time for these words, only your time. Your feelings will tell you when.

We vowed to each other on our wedding day to forsake all others till death parted us. The date of expiration of our marriage contract was death! You cannot be unfaithful now by having, holding, and not forsaking others.

Your feelings have not expired, but they are just feelings. They are important in our marriage, and yours still are, but they are not the marriage. Marriage is a commitment beyond feelings, and sometimes a commitment to endure in spite of them. And when death ends a marriage, that too happens regardless of our feelings. But you know all this. All that can remain of our marriage when I am gone is love like the desire that I wrote about in an earlier reflection. Somewhere in the Mystery of love and in the inseparable whole we are, by faith, yet connected. Our connection is in this love that endures forever, but not in married love or an expired contract broken by death. There can be no contradiction in still loving me, yet having, and holding another.

To any trace of guilt about new intimacy, know that when I am dead I cannot be jealous, selfish, or take offense. There is no greater tribute to a dead lover than that charity remains; that affection and new friendships should grow and that intimacy is not forsaken. But after you have accepted that the having and holding have expired you may still feel that the forsaking of others is still valid. My love, there is no sin in happiness or virtue in living like a goose. A goose mates for life, and if its mate dies it lives out its life unmated, as half a pair of geese. Unfortunately literature has painted glorious pictures of lovers dying in each other's arms, of lovers following their mates in death, or of lovers living on like geese. This may be good literature, but is neither good medicine nor good theology. Geese know naught of virtue nor are they commanded to love as God has commanded us.

You probably think I have gone too far, for God's command was for charity not married love. True, my love, but the glory of our marriage was that in its warmth I learned of God's love. It was hands-on love in the laboratory of marriage – experiential learning. Much of what I learned of relationships and commitment – cornerstones of charity – I learned from you. And through you I experienced both God's love and God's forgiveness. I fear that it would have been impossible for me to experience a loving God without your love. Thank you, my love. We need intimate friends to learn the lessons of love. Perhaps God throws in the passion of Eros just to keep the lessons interesting!

Sex can be void of any trace of love or caring or it can be a great source of intimacy. Ann Landers polled her readers and found that many preferred cuddling to sex. But is this surprising? For we can live without sex but without intimacy only at great emotional cost. Some men could not understand the results of her poll. How could sex, the most intimate of acts — the consummation and celebration of the sacrament of one flesh — not be preferred to cuddling? They couldn't understand because they had it figured backwards: Sex doesn't give meaning to intimacy; intimacy gives meaning to sex. Most women wanted an intimate sexual relationship, but if they had to choose between sex without intimacy and intimacy without sex, they would choose the latter. For many, lack of intimacy had already killed their joy of sex. Oh the sadness, for it can be the pleasure of lovers to choose both!

Mature children may have great difficulty in seeing their parents as sexual persons. This may become a problem for you, too. Children think their parents too old for new love — may even be repulsed by the idea. It's a trick of nature that life comes full circle. As parents influence the selection of their children's mates, children in turn may well reject a parent's new mate. Perhaps they feel that their parent is unable to make a rational decision. They are mistaken if their objection is because of age. Age does not equal senility. Nor does the need for love and intimacy grow less with age. In fact, their absence is more likely to bring an earlier death.

Who has not glimpsed an older couple holding hands? Seen fondness as they strolled along their way? Their united hands announce lessons learned – their passing grade in intimacy. Beauty matured and tested like weathered barn boards. We enjoy young lovers, but can the fickle bud compare in beauty to the fragrant flower in full blossom? Those wrinkled hands united are a privileged sight – a prayer for humankind.

Don't surrender dreams of a new relationship in all its fullness. Do not forsake your physical, mental, and spiritual health by avoiding intimacy. Shock our children for me if you must!

I am not suggesting that you should remarry. Literature has some good love stories in which a dying mate attempts to find a replacement for his lover before he dies. Such deathbed fantasies deny the reality of grief and also that of love, for within the depths of grief there is no thought of new relationships. The very love that inspires the fixing-up with a new mate would make this act a cruel joke to the other. The fantasy stems as much from guilt as love, for anyone would die more peacefully knowing that their mate would continue to be loved.

My desire is for you, my love. Not my will but yours. May you be free to live alone or again as mate. Equal options. Your free choice. The gift of love is freedom and not control. If I seem to emphasize remarriage, the reason is only this: You had no choice in being widowed. It came upon you, and may yet be lived till death without your choosing. There is no pain in a lover's vision of you remaining single if that is your free choice.

Although at present new relationships may be far from your mind, a lover asks only that you leave yourself open to consider them.

Life and love are choices for the living. I pray that you will be free to choose.

A View of Life, Love, and Self

Love knows no bounds.

Anonymous

I have almost finished writing my love-will. I think I have learned something of life and love in the process and, perhaps, it is worth including.

My desire in this reflection is to leave you with my view of love that encompasses life, death, and eternity. But one that also includes our love – a mere atom in that universal scale. But the Mystery of the whole is in that atom: omnipresent, pervasive, intimate – dwelling in our midst.

The two great commandments are to love God and to love our neighbours as ourselves. Yet the greatest social problem of our time, and probably of any time, is loneliness. Surely our greatest sin must be to collapse inward in a miniature imitation of a cosmic collapsing universe: our growth decreasing till we finally stagnate, then regress with increasing rate till we collapse upon ourselves in our own shrinking world of isolation and indifference.

Although many people vibrantly radiate love, far too many lose the Mystery of love along their way and without it their world shrinks. Like stunted trees they are the twisted and deformed that grow among the firmly rooted, tall, full trees that stand in splendid support of life even when old and mossy.

The old adage seems true. However we bend in life we eventually grow. We expand into Heaven or shrink into Hell. C. S. Lewis described Hell in *The Great Divorce* as a place where people lived in vast isolation. But even with a bus service to Heaven, they could only visit because their own shrunken lives kept them doomed to Hell.

Scientists sharpen their pencils and recalculate the mass of the universe. Does it have sufficient momentum to continue expanding or will gravity eventually make it collapse? In our micro-imitation, our pencil is reflective prayer, the momentum is love, and the force of gravity is the weight of our sins against love. Will our growth continue so that with God's grace we escape our worldly bounds to an eternity of infinite love? Or will the weight of our sins against love become too strong and pull us back? This importance of love is central to my view of life. And how I pray that we may retain this sense of love and, with the grace of God, gain escape velocity.

In writing this love-will I tried to put myself and my cares aside. I wanted to be selfless and to be present for you as a perfect gift. I considered writing without an "I," but failed in my opening words. One does not vanish through unselfish love but, instead, becomes more visible. Being selfless may prevent selfishness but love requires giving of self. Upon rereading, I find that I have scattered myself on every page.

I pray that my words are not egocentric. Please accept that I could not write about love without also celebrating and mourning. I celebrated because love intensified my desire to share myself with you by writing long reflections, sharing counsel, and giving freely of my hopes, dreams and fears. That is the celebrating part of unselfish love – free giving of self. But even this celebrated sharing of self has a spiritual parallel, for there are none who love God better than those who share themselves openly with Him through reflective prayer. Our Father dances for joy!

But I also mourn, for all lovers mourn. It is an inseparable part of loving. As I try to write with perfect love, I glimpse Perfect Love more clearly. But in these moments I mourned my failures, for to glimpse even dimly the Mystery of love calls me to mourn my own unloving. I used to think confessionals were filled with sinners but I peeked through a crack in their secret place and saw only lovers whispering in the darkness.

And so, my love, I write of unselfish love, and yet inseparable is my celebrating and my mourning. But this unites us, for it must be the same for you in your grief. However good our lives may be, we would still grieve like Yahweh grieved. Take comfort that God grieves – that grief unites all lovers.

Much of love I learned from you. Your love is important and so are you. I want to convince you of that in my love-will. I tried to capture some of our love and freely return it to help you through your grief. This love will not be lost, for it is merely a part of eternal love. When I die our love will undergo a metamorphosis, but it will not die except through failure to love others. I pray that these words give love a boost both for you and for others whom your life may touch. May your love for me grow to something new, ever carry you onward and outward till its infinite meaning is found in eternity.

The Eternity of Love

*Natural loves can hope for eternity only in so
far as they have allowed themselves to be taken
into the eternity of Charity . . .*

C. S. Lewis

I have just finished reading *The Four Loves* in which C.S. Lewis
writes beautifully about surrendering natural loves for eternal
love. One day we will have to give up our natural love for
something more. You may need to relinquish your dream of an
exclusive union in paradise. Perhaps I seem cruel in writing of
this separation, for thoughts of such a union may be comforting in your grief. But this final separation in the last stage of
grief is different. It's the wide-eyed child dropping her love-
tattered teddy bear on Christmas morning so she can accept
more gifts. Our faith urges us to release our exclusive union so
that ultimately we may accept much more in the wholeness of
Mystery.

I write about this separation because friends may use the promise of future union to comfort you. Indeed, the simplicity of the promise is comforting so by all means accept it. But it could come to cause you problems. If you crawl away into a corner to savour our union you will later find that you are alone in an empty corner. It is this vision that makes a lover write of eternity. In death our union will not be exclusive, as is our married love, but all-inclusive like charity. C. S. Lewis expressed this beautifully in *The Four Loves*:

In heaven there will be no anguish and no duty of turning away from our earthly beloveds. First, because we shall have turned already; from the portraits to the Original, from the rivulets to the Fountain, from the creatures He made lovable to Love Himself. But secondly, because we shall find them all in Him. By loving Him more than them we shall love them more than we now do.

Beautiful! Yet, the truth for you in your grief will be the converse: On earth there is no need to force ourselves to hang onto departed lovers. First, because we are already firmly attached; to the portraits in the Original, to the rivulets in the Fountain, to the beloveds in the Lover. But secondly, because we shall find wholeness and Mystery in all our worldly friends. By loving them more than departed lovers, we shall love the departed lovers more because they have been embraced into the Mystery of love and wholeness.

I do not wish to make our married love sound unimportant, for however imperfect, it is an image of divine love. The original is the whole Mystery of God. Christianity does not promise an exclusive relationship with me, but much more with God. And so I pray that I have presented our love in all its richness, yet have not idolized it. Our married love will end when I die and will not be reborn. What this truth means for you, my love, is that when I am gone your union with me will be through loving others. It will not be in withholding but in giving! Our union that grew because it was exclusive, will grow by being inclusive. This is why a love-will, whatever the initial intention, turns to talking, writing, praying, friendship, and celebrating. It must embrace life.

If I seem to dwell on Christian themes it is only because I find no greater comfort than our faith and the promise of eternal love. And also, as I write, examples from the greatest love story of all time come readily to mind. At first I attempted to moderate my spiritual words. In the end I found that I could do no better than totally give myself as every lover must. Not to convert or change you, but as a gift.

I have written to give you comfort. I have written also to help you separate from me with your inheritance intact so you may invest it in others. I am sure, my love, that we will experience a mysterious connection in the hereafter, but please don't dwell on it. Whatever our connection may be, it cannot be lost now no matter whom or how you love. I must now, by faith, be united with God. If so, I will be closest to you when you forget me in the loving of others. Have faith. I celebrate your loving legacy as you build it, and I will celebrate it with you forever in Paradise.

Good-bye, My Love

. . . there are two you's,
the one you create
by loving
and the one the beloved creates
by loving you.

Robert Penn Warren

The law office phoned to say that our legal wills have been revised as we had directed and are ready for us to sign. I will say good-bye now so our lawyer can seal my love-will in his safe with my legal will. I hope it is a very long time before it is needed and I don't want it to get lost.

Parting is difficult for us even when it is only for a few days. We share a hug and a kiss as we leave the house but do so again at the airport. We even have a quick kiss at the parting gate. Now I am at the parting gate, for this is the closing section of my love-will. As I make this final good-bye, I want to give you several lingering hugs and kisses.

Thank you for loving me. The love expressed in this love-will is only a poor reflection of the love you gave me and of what I learned by loving you. All I have given you was first of all your gift to me in our marriage. For this gift above all else, I thank you. I pray that I have acknowledged your gift and returned it for your comfort in this my love-will.

It is easy to accept that love gives meaning to our life. It's more difficult to accept that love equally gives meaning to a loved one's death and to our grief. I pray that my love-will helps you accept this meaning, for the God of love is always the same — steadfast and unconditional. Our love would be without unity and meaning if this love were not reality.

Some people may well wonder why I would write a love-will that may remind you of our love instead of letting you forget and get on with your life. They do not know the paradox unless they themselves have grieved. While it is lost love we grieve, love is the ultimate meaning that makes grief bearable. So, I have given you the gift of our love not for you to grieve it more, but to give meaning and healing to your grief.

If one has loved enough to grieve then that love is also strong enough to give meaning to the grief. Perhaps this is why grief will heal unless it is infected by regrets, doubts, blame, guilt, and the many other diseases of honest grief. This also is why I have written: Love is a disinfectant that protects the open wound of grief so it can heal without infection.

If love were split into two parts, what would the healing

comfort of love say to the grieving hurt of love? I have struggled for the words, but grasped only a shadow of love. Yet, I
have glimpsed the Unconditional First Love, the Great Com-
forter, Mystery. I hope that my inadequate words have shown
the eternal God of love and you find these words comforting.
My prayer is that you have seen love in the midst of death and,
that in some small way, I have helped you to accept love in
your grief – helped you to love in your grief and thus to love
life. I pray that your capacity to love has grown, for love is forever an onward journey with no turning back – a calling out of
our wilderness, whatever its name.

Love is also freedom and so I pray that I have helped you
let go of me without letting go of love. I pray that you accept
my gift of our love and that it helps you to embrace love and to
grow in love even through your grief. All beginnings are born
out of endings.

And now I must say good-bye, but not a final good-bye
because we must accept on faith that love never ends and that
one day, in some way that we cannot imagine, we will meet
again. For now, I have done what I set out to do – to complete
our business of love and to say farewell.

My love-will called me in the midst of our marriage to
look beyond to a time when we would become separate. As I
complete my love-will, I think that the words of love are the
best that I have ever written, but I pray that you will not have

the occasion to read them. I also pray that I will not lose you, but it is unlikely that we will die together. You *are* reading my love-will, which means that the laws of statistics that predicted that you would outlive me proved to be true. My hope and prayer for you is that I have lighted your road and helped you continue the dance of life.

Only you will know how long my love-will remained locked away. If it seems timeless and to have truly come from beyond my grave, it is because grief itself is universal and timeless. A specter of grief yawned open before me, as I am sure it does for most lovers. I have written what love called me to write to comfort what I have seen. I must now say good-bye.

You have read my love-will with your eyes. I ask you to reread it with your heart and to complete what you must do to say good-bye to me also. My lover's wish is that you continue to live abundantly, to grow, and to love. I pray that in some way my loving you has made a difference – that it has left you more able to love, for that is the urging of the Mystery of life.

I leave you now with love and my prayers always. I realize that beyond my rambling words, my love-will has been a prayer for you, for in its essence a love-will can be nothing more than a statement of desire.

I can do no more than to leave you now in the hands of Love. God be with you now and always. "There are three things that remain – faith, hope and love – and the greatest of these is love." Good-bye.

A Summary of My Desire

May Yahweh bless you and keep you.
May Yahweh let his face shine on you and be
gracious to you.
May Yahweh uncover his face to you and bring
you peace.

Numbers 6:24–26

My desire is that my love-will:

- is true to the spirit of love and to our married life
- is respectful of your personhood and reverent to your creation
- is non-possessive and liberating
- is helpful to you in owning your feelings and making them your friends
- helps you feel good about yourself and your past
- restores a healthy ambition so that work affirms you and gives you pleasure
- delights in your creating
- gives hope to sustain you

- helps lead you to mental and spiritual wholeness
- restores your confidence whatever the future may bring
- helps you find your new identity
- restores happiness in the depths of your being
- allows you growth without being controlled by change
- inspires you with a sense of awe and a reverence for life
- helps you feel that you belong
- continues to affirm you
- frees you to make your choices in love and life
- leaves you a quiet space for peaceful restoration
- prepares you to invest in new friends and to richly live in love
- helps you find your strength
- helps you feel the spirit of Incarnate Love in you.

Epilogue

Nothing finally is final —
every love is a rain
opening the bud to fire
asking and receiving its own Easter.

Phyllis Webb

I have retrieved my dusty love-will from its niche in time. The passing years have not dated my words of love. I have read the yellowed pages a dozen times, for my love is dead and it is I who grieve. All that I once foresaw has come to rest with me. I did not know when I wrote to comfort a lover's grief that my words would comfort me.

How slow I was to understand that love and grief are one. Every lover must bear his grief and every grief is born in love. There is a lover and a griever, inseparable, in us all. It does not matter to my comfort that I wrote the words of love. Whether written to my love, or to any grieving lover, the meaning of love is the same as are one's needs in grief.

Would the love-will of my love have been so very different? Like spouses' wills that are mirror images to provide for each other's needs, their love-wills would be just variations on a theme. But love-wills would be more similar still than ordinary wills, for wills deal with things that are bought and sold, that may be separately owned, whereas a love-will deals with the bond itself. What was between lovers will always be. It shapes us to our graves and by our faith beyond. And so I know, from the truth of love, that the words could not be more hers if it were her hand that set them to the pages.

I thank the words that console me in my grief. I know the words are of my love. They speak of purpose; they give me life, and that was truly her. For others like me, who would write a love-will to comfort grief, keep ever in your mind that your words may well be for yourself. Know, too, that such a will speaks more of life than death, for there is, by faith, no death in love.

Acknowledgments

I am indebted to all the people who loved me enough to make this book possible. I especially thank my wife, Colleen, who was unfailingly supportive, encouraging and helpful. I also thank our friends in the Guelph Image Group who over the past twenty years shared their friendship and their commitment to marriage.

A special thanks to Marilyn Gostlin, Lenore Latta, Marianne Micros, Susan and Steven Scadding, Rosaleen and Peter Tomblin, and Reverend Fritz Schmidt for encouragement and helpful reviews.

I sincerely thank my editors, Maryjean Lancefield and Maya Mavjee, who helped me create a book from a collection of love letters, and my publisher, Ed Boyce, and Moulin Publishing for believing in me and launching this book.

One or more of the quotations that begin each section were drawn from the *Columbia Dictionary of Quotations*, *The Dictionary of Canadian Quotations and Phrases*, *Dictionary of Quotations*, *Encyclopedia of Religious Quotations*, *Quotations by Women* and *The Whole World Book of Quotations*.

I thank the following sources for the remaining quotations: Atwood, Margaret, *The Handmaid's Tale* (McClelland and Stewart/Bantam Limited, 1985); Burns, George, *Gracie: a love story* (Putnam Books, 1988); Buscaglia, Leo F., *Living, Loving & Learning* (Charles B. Slack, Inc., 1982); Caine, Lynn, *Being a Widow* (Arbor House, 1988); Cassem, Ned. H., "The First Three Steps Beyond the Grave" in *Acute Grief and the Funeral* (Charles C. Thomas – Publisher, 1976); Cowper, William, "Mutual Forbearance Necessary to the Happiness of the Married State" in *The Poetical Works of William Cowper* (Ballantyne Press); Goldberg, Natalie, *Writing Down the Bones* (Shambhala, 1986); Kalish, Richard A., *Death, Grief, and Caring Relationships* (Brooks/Cole Publishing Company, 1981); Lewis, C. S., *The Four Loves* (Fontana Books, 1960); May, Rollo, *Man's Search for Himself* (W. W. Norton & Company, Inc., 1953); Nouwen, Henri J. M., *Reaching Out: The Three Movements of the Spiritual life* (Doubleday & Company, Inc., 1975); Seeland, Irene B., "The Funeral as a Therapeutic Tool in Acute Bereavement" in *Acute Grief* (Columbia University Press, 1981); Staudacher, Carol, *Beyond Grief: a guide for recovering from the death of a loved one* (New Harbinger Publications, 1987); Tatelbaum, Judy, *The Courage to Grieve* (Lippincott & Crowell, 1980); Vanauken, Sheldon, *A Severe Mercy* (Harper & Row, 1977).